Commandments for

Christian Living

Douglas Beyer

Judson Press ® Valley Forge

Library of Congress Cataloging in Publication Data
Beyer, Douglas.
    Commandments for Christian living.

    Includes bibliographical references.
    1. Ten commandments. 2. Christian life—1960-
I. Title.
BV4655.B45 1983   241.5'2   83-12008
ISBN 0-8170-1008-4

To
Mom and Dad
Who by Precept and Example
First Taught Me
The Commandments for Christian Living

Contents

Introduction

In my first book, *Basic Beliefs of Christians,* I attempted to present a broad perspective of what Christians have believed through the ages and across national and denominational boundaries. *Commandments for Christian Living* tries to set forth a universal moral code based on the commandments of Moses and Jesus. Christianity has both a creed of doctrine and a code of conduct, a system of belief and a system of behavior. It demands both orthodoxy and orthopraxy, straight thinking and straight living.

In the ancient Greco-Roman world, philosophers taught a system of ethics, and priests taught the myths of the gods. But the gods weren't moral, and the ethics weren't godly. The Hebrew prophets, on the other hand, by divine revelation brought both God and ethics together: Yahweh was the source of moral law. Moses introduced the Ten Commandments with this authoritative word: "God spoke, and these were his words . . ." (Exodus 20:1).

God has spoken, but humankind hasn't listened. We have made many attempts to dodge our moral obligations. The moral crisis of our time is not just the widespread violation of accepted moral standards but also the denial that there are any such standards. The very notion of a binding moral code seems to be losing its meaning for many men and women today. To violate moral standards while at the same time acknowledging their authority is one thing, but to lose all sense of transcendent obligation and to repudiate all moral authority is something far more serious. To be lost on the freeway is bad enough, but to throw the map out the window is worse. And to argue at length that maps don't exist is the worst condition imaginable.

Some people try to draw their own moral maps. The ancient individualist ethic, which holds that morality is a matter of individual, private, personal judgment, has been revived. Denying that there is a law-giver to whom they must give an account, some people prefer to make up their own rules. Their naturalistic philosophy makes it impossible for them to distinguish between "I ought to pray" and "I feel like praying"; to them "I ought" is the same sort of statement as "I itch."

Others attempt to avoid the demands of God's laws by appealing to biblical proof texts that seem to abolish it. They may quote Romans 6:14, ". . . You do not live under law but under God's grace," but they fail to go on to the next verse, "What, then? Shall we sin, because we are not under law but under God's grace? By no means!" Paul seems to be addressing the very ones who say that grace permits any kind of behavior. Grace does not give license to sin; grace gives power to overcome sin and break its dominion.

Jesus said, "Do not think that I have come to do away with the Law of Moses and the teachings of the prophets. I have not come to do away with them, but to make their teachings come true" (Matthew 5:17). Paul asks, "Does this mean that by this faith we do away with the Law?" and then answers, "No, not at all; instead we uphold the Law" (Romans 3:31). Later he says, ". . . The Law itself is holy, and the commandment is holy, right, and good" (Romans 7:12).

Yet it is not enough to say that the law is good. What is it good for? To that question there are three answers, three good uses to which the law is put. The first function of the law is *political*. It serves as a restraint of evil in society. "We know that the Law is good if it is used as it should be used. It must be remembered, of course, that laws are made, not for good people, but for lawbreakers and criminals, for the godless and sinful . . ." (1 Timothy 1:8-9). The law will not save a person from his or her sins, but it may save others from his or her sins. Its purpose is to preserve society from moral disintegration.

The second function of the law is *theological*. It serves as an agent to reveal humankind's sinful condition and to lead persons to Christ. "The law was our schoolmaster [paidagogos] to bring us unto Christ, that we might be justified by faith" (Galatians 3:24, KJV). The law is a chaperone. In ancient Greece and Rome the chaperone was a slave who escorted a child to school and back. He had no authority to control the child's behavior, no authority to punish, and no authority to instruct;

he had only the authority to report the child's misbehavior. This is a higher view of law than the merely political view. A political view of law leads to legalism in religion, but a high view leads the lawbreaker to seek divine grace.

The third function of the law is *didactic*. It serves as a guide for the regenerate who has responded to God's grace in repentance and faith: Paul says, "We ask God to fill you with the knowledge of his will, with all the wisdom and understanding that his Spirit gives. Then you will be able to live as the Lord wants and will always do what pleases him" (Colossians 1:9-10). Love is the motive of Christian behavior. Horatius Bonar, writer of the beloved hymn, "I Heard the Voice of Jesus Say," wrote,

> But will they tell us what is to regulate service, if not law? *Love,* they say. This is pure fallacy. Love is not a *rule,* but a *motive*. Love does not tell me *what* to do; it tells me *how* to do it. Love constrains me to do the will of the beloved one; but to know what that will is I must go elsewhere. The law of our God is *the will* of the beloved one. . . .[1]

Jesus said, "If ye love me, keep my commandments" (John 14:15, KJV).

Although Christians are redeemed by grace through faith, they remain sinners (1 John 1:8) and, therefore, continue to hear the accusations of the law. But now they see the law in another light, as God's loving will.

> . . . They find joy in obeying
> the Law of the LORD,
> and they study it day and
> night.
> —Psalm 1:2

For them the commandments are not bars on a cage but rafters in a roof that shelters from the storms of life.

"When all else fails, try reading the instructions" is good advice whether one is trying to assemble a lawn mower or a life. Are there instructions for putting life together so that everything fits with no left-over parts? Is there a manufacturer's maintenance manual for the human psyche? Yes! The most basic list of instructions was given to humankind by God in the holy Scriptures. The Decalogue and the multiplication table go back far into history, but neither is old-fashioned or out of date. No other code of law has grasped the mind of humankind and influenced behavior so widely and for so long as the Ten Commandments. Even people who no longer believe in God profess to honor the Ten Commandments, the touchstone of ethics for over three thousand years.

In this book, I will attempt to avoid marginal issues and cultural mores in order to get back to the basic behavior of Christians as it is declared in the great commandments of Moses and Jesus. At the end of each chapter of this book you will find a systematic arrangement of biblical references for further study.

Note: The use of the masculine gender in referring to God throughout this book and in the Bible does not deny God's feminine characteristics. God has been revealed as both Father (John 5:17-23) and Mother (Isaiah 49:15). Jesus likens God to a shepherd who rejoices when *he* finds a lost sheep (Luke 15:3-7) and to a woman who rejoices when *she* finds a lost coin (Luke 15:8-10). The personality is important, not the sexuality. "I am God and not man [or woman] . . ." (Hosea 11:9).

1

Worship Only the
One True God

Morality, like art, consists of the ability to draw a line somewhere. The first issue to deal with, however, is not *where* to draw the line, but *who* draws it. If humankind draws it, humankind can move it or erase it. Some people, for instance, think they can make up their own rules of behavior. Resenting any moral code imposed by someone else, they imagine that they are the only ones who can decide what's right or what's wrong. So they design an ethical system to be the way they like it.

However, if God is the One who draws the line, people can no more make up the moral laws of God than they can make up the natural laws of physics. The same God who made both laws *gives* them to humankind. People can't amend or repeal a single one. The God who gave life also gave the laws by which to live. Humankind's job, then, is not to design a system but to discover God's.

Thus, the Ten Commandments begin with an important word from the Sponsor: "I am the LORD your God who brought you out of Egypt, where you were slaves. Worship no god but me."

Here's Something to Do

The First Commandment appears to be obsolete. When was the last time you were seriously tempted to worship Baal or to offer incense to Jupiter or to drink a toast to Bacchus or to sacrifice a lamb to Zeus? Where have all the idols gone? Has the great Yahweh licked all competition? Do people need only nine commandments nowadays?

Times have changed since Moses brought the tablets down from Mt. Sinai. The world seems to have moved from polytheism to monotheism to atheism—from the worship of many gods to the worship of one God to the worship of no God. Old-fashioned pagans had to choose between a chaotic universe alive with lawless gods and an ordered universe under the one Yahweh and his moral law. Modern pagans choose between that divine order and the flat, fortuitous, fatalistic universe of atheism. This choice is usually made without knowing it—not by clear conviction but by vague drifting, not by denying God but by losing interest in God.

The twentieth century religious sophisticate says, "Of course, there may be some sort of higher power that created the world, but it's childish to suppose that it has any personal relation to me!" In such a creed lie the germs of an undiagnosed atheism. "The man who says, 'One God,' and does not *care,*" Joy Davidman claims, "is an atheist in his heart." [1]

We might have expected the First Commandment to say "Thou shalt believe in God," a commandment against atheism. But God took care of that in creation. God created each of us with an emptiness in our souls that can be filled only with God. No one has to teach a baby to be hungry or thirsty. Instead, one teaches the baby how to satisfy that hunger and thirst. Although nothing less than God can fully satisfy the hunger of our beings, many people still waste their lives foolishly seeking idolatrous substitutes. Idolatry is the junk food of the soul. Junk food may temporarily sate the appetite, but it does not nourish the body. Fifteen hundred years ago Augustine prayed, "Thou has formed us for Thyself, and our hearts are restless till they find rest in Thee." [2]

To worship any god other than the one true God leads not only to spiritual famine but also to slavery. No substitute god is big enough to sustain the commitment of a person's life. World history is filled with sad tales of victims who have first-class loyalty to second-class causes that failed them. Whatever a person worships, regardless of its name, is that person's god. To worship anything is to treat it as being the greatest thing in life, the center around which the rest of a person's interests revolve. Locate whatever it is that a person acts toward in this way, and you have named that person's god. It is his or her functional theology regardless of what creed is professed.

If a person's life is centered on something too small, he or she will be running in circles instead of orbiting the great universe that God made and of which he himself is the center and axis. Worship of the one true God expands life and enables a person to experience and enjoy the whole of it. Worship of anything less than God constricts and enslaves. Theologically, a person may profess faith in the God who made humankind

while at the same time psychologically be controlled and dominated by
the gods he or she makes.

Here's Something to Avoid

The Bible frequently reminds us that God is a jealous God, who will
not share affection with rivals (Exodus 34:14; Deuteronomy 4:24; 5:9;
Joshua 24:19). God loves us too much to stand idly by while we go
"whoring" after other gods that will only disappoint and destroy us
(Exodus 34:15-16; Ezekiel 16:1-43; Hosea 4:12; 9:1). The substitute
gods bear many names. We will consider only three of the most common:
self, sex, and security.

The God of Self

Modern idolators are in greater need of the First Commandment than
their ancient counterparts who were at least worshiping something other
than themselves, a power greater than themselves. The primitive poly-
theists were intending to serve God. The modern monotheists, however,
often mistake their own mirror images for deity. Instead of saying,
"Unto me, a sinner, God has spoken," they say by implication, "When
I speak, God agrees." They worship themselves with all their hearts,
strength, souls and minds, and themselves only do they serve.

The apostle Paul describes those who worship "self" as people "whose
God is their belly" (Philippians 3:19, KJV). Or to change the metaphor
to something more elegant, English teacher C. S. Lewis says that such
self-worshipers are adjectives trying to act like nouns.[3] People (adjectives) were created to depend on and relate to God, but self-worshipers
seek to become autonomous and self-existent (nouns).

"Self," like all idols, however, makes promises it can't keep. However much its service satisfies for the moment, ultimately it disappoints.
"Eat, drink, and be merry," self proclaims, "for tomorrow we die."
But just how merry can one be when one's mind is haunted by that fatal
tomorrow? Living for one's own pleasure is the least pleasurable thing
that a person can do. If one's neighbors don't kill him or her in disgust,
he or she will die slowly of boredom and loneliness. Self-worship is the
only religion in which the more devoted a person is, the fewer proselytes
he or she makes.

God can do little with a person who is self-satisfied or self-confident.
God cannot possess the self-possessed. He is able to do something great
through a person only when he or she feels utterly inadequate for the
job.

The God of Sex

The god of sex has really "been around." Ancient Canaanites called the god Ashtoreth; the Greeks called it Aphrodite; and the Romans called it Venus. The god changes its name and image, but the same lusts that stirred the ancients to the worship of sex still move in people's hearts today. The problem in saying any words of warning about this idol is that it has such admirable and attractive qualities that its devotees think the prophet of Yahweh is being mean-spirited in his or her warnings. Let it be clear at the outset that the god of sex, like all false gods, is a fallen *angel*. Sex was created by the one true God and intended for people's good pleasure. But when sex is misused, when other values are sacrificed to it, and when it is worshiped supremely, it delivers misery and debauchery. Sexuality is not something inherently bad; it is something good. And for that very reason people are tempted to idolize it, giving it the devotion that belongs only to God.

No idol betrays its worshipers so quickly and obviously as the god of sex; no other false god makes greater promises and fails so painfully. The sexual revolution of the midtwentieth century, which promised to cure people's Victorian sexual hang-ups, has created, in fact, a worse situation. It has left in its wake more unwanted pregnancies, more venereal disease, and more broken homes, broken hearts, and broken lives than plagued our hung-up forebears.

The God of Security

Devotees of the god of security believe that faith is a poor substitute for money on deposit. Their aim is to acquire enough worldly goods so that they won't have to trust God any longer for their "daily bread."

Jesus called the god of security "mammon." The root meaning of the word is "trust." It was a good word. Originally it referred to what one entrusted to a banker or friend. Later it came to mean "that in which one puts trust." And finally, mammon was recognized as an idol, that which is trusted instead of God. How far the angel has fallen!

As long as people consider all of their worldly goods simply as matters entrusted to them by the Real Owner, people are responsible stewards. But the moment people place their trust in goods instead of the One who gave them, people become idolaters.

If offered a clear-cut alternative of giving up God or possessions, most of us, I hope, would choose God. But the choice is rarely put that bluntly. Subconsciously people often make decisions which show that their real commitment is to things, not to God. Security, national or personal, is the real basis of all decisions, the pivotal point of people's dedication. When the chips are down, people would rather have gold than God. Aaron led the Israelites to melt down their earrings to make the golden calf. In our time, people worship gold without melting it.

Jesus did not say that people must serve God *more* than money but that people must serve God *or* money (Luke 16:13). It's Yahweh or mammon; take your pick! Although Americans stamp their coins "In God We Trust," they often mean "In This God We Trust." People either serve God and use money or serve money and use God.

The god of security is deceitful and its bondage subtle. It is like the flypaper and the fly: the fly lands on the sticky substance, thinking, *My flypaper,* only to discover that the flypaper is saying, *My fly.* Be careful lest your possessions possess you. Those who pursue the god of security are condemned to perpetual and ultimate insecurity. Someday even the most securely wealthy will hear God say, "You fool! This very night you will have to give up your life; then who will get all these things you have kept for yourself?" (Luke 12:20).

Humankind is incurably religious. We must worship something. We cannot not worship. Our only choice is to choose which god we will worship. We are free to pick which god will control our lives; we are free to choose whether our veins will flow with God's red blood or the pus of idols. To paraphrase the great Joshua: Choose you this day whom you will serve, whether the true and living God of your ancestors or the gods of self, sex, and security, the gods of those in whose land you dwell. But as for me and my house, we will serve the Lord (Joshua 24:15).

Scripture References for Further Study

Ancient Jews Followed the Foreign Gods:

Of the Egyptians   *Joshua 24:14; Ezekiel 23:3-19; Acts 7:39-41*
Of the Moabites   *Numbers 25:1-3*
Of the Canaanites   *Judges 2:11-13; 1 Chronicles 5:25*
Of the Assyrians   *Ezekiel 16:28-30; 23:5-7*

Idolatry Consists of:

Looking to other gods   *Hosea 3:1*
Swearing by other gods   *Exodus 23:13, KJV; Joshua 23:7*
Walking after other gods   *Deuteronomy 8:19, KJV*
Speaking in the name of other gods   *Deuteronomy 18:20*

Fearing other gods   2 Kings 17:35, KJV
Sacrificing to other gods   Exodus 22:20
Worshiping
  angels   Deuteronomy 4:19, KJV; 17:3, KJV; Colossians 2:18
  the devil, demons   Matthew 4:9-10; Revelation 9:20
  dead people   1 Samuel 28:13-14; Psalm 106:28
  moon and stars   Deuteronomy 4:19; 17:3; 2 Kings 23:5; Acts 7:42
Desiring things
  contrary to God's will   Colossians 3:5-7; 1 Peter 4:2-3
  to feed selfish appetites   Philippians 3:18-19

Idolatry Is Described as:

Useless   Judges 10:14; Psalm 115:4-8; Isaiah 44:19; Jeremiah 10:3-5
Foolish   Acts 17:29; Romans 1:21-23
Abominable   Deuteronomy 7:25, KJV; 16:22; Jeremiah 44:4-5, KJV

Those Who Practice Idolatry:

Forsake God   2 Kings 22:17, KJV; Jeremiah 16:11, KJV
Forget God   Deuteronomy 8:19; Jeremiah 18:15
Go astray from God   Ezekiel 14:5; 44:10, KJV; 1 Corinthians 12:2
Dishonor the name of God   Ezekiel 20:39
Provoke God   Deuteronomy 31:20, KJV; Isaiah 65:3; Jeremiah 25:6
Are ignorant and foolish   Romans 1:21-23, KJV
Are proud of it   Psalm 97:7, KJV
Are carried away by it   1 Corinthians 12:2, KJV
Suffer captivity   2 Kings 17:5-23

With Respect to Idolatry Saints Should:

Flee from idolatry   1 Corinthians 10:14
Keep from worshiping false gods   Joshua 23:7; 1 John 5:21
Have nothing associated with idols in their homes   Deuteronomy 7:26
Avoid relationships with those who worship idols
  in religion   Joshua 23:7; 1 Corinthians 5:11
  in alliances   Exodus 34:12, 15; Deuteronomy 7:2
  in marriage   Exodus 34:16; Deuteronomy 7:3

Idolatry Is Punished by:

Suffering   Jeremiah 16:1-13
Banishment   Jeremiah 8:3; Hosea 10:5-8; Amos 5:26-27
Death   Deuteronomy 17:2-5

Hell   *1 Corinthians 6:9-10; Ephesians 5:5; Revelation 14:9-11; Revelation 21:8; 22:15*

Rewards of Right Worship:

The house of worship
  is the locus of God's presence   *2 Chronicles 7:15-16*
  is the means of God's blessing   *Psalm 65:4*
  is the end of human longing   *Psalm 84:1-4, 10*
Fruitful living   *Psalm 92:13-14*

2

Worship the True God Only in the Right Way

Worship is commonly considered a harmless activity. In many people's opinions, worship is as bland as mashed potatoes. However, consider the possibility that it might be highly dangerous. Certainly in the mind of those who drew up the first biblical code of moral law, it ranked right up there with important matters such as murder, theft, and adultery. Of the ten commandments that God gave, the first two deal with worship. To worship, therefore, is to engage in risky business. At the very least, one is liable to transgress the law of God.

People nowadays feel less guilty about breaking the first two commandments than they feel about breaking the other eight, but the Bible has more to say about the Second Commandment than any of the rest.

> Do not make for yourselves images of anything in heaven or on earth or in the water under the earth. Do not bow down to any idol or worship it, because I am the LORD your God and I tolerate no rivals. I bring punishment on those who hate me and on their descendants down to the third and fourth generation. But I show my love to thousands of generations of those who love me and obey my laws (Exodus 20:4-6).

The commandment has two parts: do not make images, and do not bow down to images. Three reasons are given for this commandment: (1) God will tolerate no rivals; (2) God will bring punishment on those who hate God; and (3) God will show love to thousands who love God and obey the law. In other words, it is important how a person worships God, because he is the only God who makes a difference in life. If God makes no difference, if God does not love and hate, punish and reward, then who does care how or whether one worships God? Worship has been trivialized because people have no awareness of how it matters to the great Yahweh.

What This Commandment Means

It is not enough merely to avoid worshiping false gods as the First Commandment prescribes; people must worship the true God in the right way. The intent of the Second Commandment is to emphasize this. This commandment clearly demolishes the popular notion that as long as someone is sincere, God is pleased with any kind of worship. The issue raised here is not will one worship the right God, but will one worship him in the right way. Specifically, one's worship must be without images.

Images of the true God are as much forbidden as are images of false gods. Aaron's first big mistake occurred over this point. While his brother Moses was on the mountain receiving the law, Aaron was down in the valley making a golden calf out of the earrings that the Israelites had asked for from the Egyptians (Exodus 12:35). The golden calf was expressly dedicated as a representation of Yahweh. Aaron and his cohorts would have been shocked if anyone had suggested that they were worshiping a *foreign* god. The people said, "This is our god, who led us out of Egypt," and they called a festival to "honor the LORD" (Exodus 32:1-5). But God said that the people had sinned and rejected him. The image may have borne his name, but he knew it was not him that the people worshiped.

Even religious treasures can become idols when they divert attention from God. The bronze serpent that God told Moses to make in the wilderness and used to heal the Israelites from snake bites (Numbers 21:9) and that became a symbol of Christ's saving power (John 3:14-15) was worshiped as an idol and had to be destroyed by Hezekiah (2 Kings 18:4).

It is by God's mercy that we don't have a single original manuscript signed by an apostle or prophet. If we did, we would surely turn it into an idol, focusing not on what it said but on the thing itself. Recently a great deal of interest has been aroused in trying to verify the Shroud of Turin as the burial clothes of Jesus. Frankly, even if it is the actual garment that our Lord wore in the tomb, I hope that can't be proven. The temptation would be overwhelming for people to give more reverent attention to Jesus' burial clothes than to the risen Lord. We are fortunate that we have no ark of the covenant, no temple, and no relic of Jesus and the apostles. Our worship must focus on God alone and not on the things God used through history to make himself known.

To deal with the chronic temptation of turning the *means* of worship into the *end* of worship thus corrupting the act of worship, God commanded, "Do not make for yourselves images of anything. . . ." Although that appears to be absolute and unqualified, further reading of the Bible shows that making images is not totally forbidden. What is forbidden is making images that serve as objects of worship. Immediately after the commandment was given, God ordered Israel to make two golden cherubim as part of the ark of the Covenant to be placed in the tabernacle (Exodus 25:18). This point was missed by Jews who, Joy Davidman notes, "have accomplished so much with music and literature [but] have done almost nothing with sculpture and painting." [1]

Jews weren't the only ones to miss the point. Back in the eighth century wars broke out between Christians over the interpretation of the Second Commandment. The Iconoclasts (Yes, that was their real name; the word means "image breaker.") demanded that all images be eliminated from worship. They won the first round with the Council of Constantinople, A.D. 726–754, but lost their point with the second Council of Nicea, A.D. 754–787. To this day the Eastern Orthodox Church confines images to colored representations on a flat surface while the Roman Catholic Church allows sculptured images. Neither measure, of course, gets at the core of the issue: the attitude of the worshiper. An image is but a solid metaphor. Any metaphor—sculptured, painted, written, or spoken—can become an idol when it is treated as holy in itself, as though it contains undiluted deity.

C. S. Lewis suggests this "Footnote to All Prayers."

> He whom I bow to only knows to whom I bow
> When I attempt the ineffable Name, murmuring *Thou,*
> And dream of Pheidian fancies and embrace in heart
> Symbols (I know) which cannot be the thing Thou art.
> Thus always, taken at their word, all prayers blaspheme
> Worshipping with frail images a folk-lore dream,
> And all men in their praying, self-deceived, address
> The coinage of their own unquiet thoughts, unless
> Thou in magnetic mercy to Thyself divert
> Our arrows, aimed unskilfully, beyond desert;
> And all men are idolators, crying unheard
> To a deaf idol, if Thou take them at their word.
>
> Take not, oh Lord, our literal sense. Lord, in Thy great,
> Unbroken speech our limping metaphor translate. [2]

We can't dismiss image making as an ancient superstition that we have long since outgrown. No institution or custom as universal as idolatry is founded wholly on superstition (or falsehood). "If it does not answer some real human need, if its foundations are not laid broad and deep in the nature of things, it must perish. . . ."[3] Image making has human need behind it and human nature beneath it.

Consider how it operates in a contemporary situation. The wife of a prisoner of war keeps a picture of her husband in a prominent place in her home. It serves as a cherished reminder of her beloved in his absence. But when he returns, she puts the picture aside and gives full attention to him. And, what is most important, she *allows him to be different* than her memory and picture portray.

The church, "Bride of Christ," needs the same good judgment about all its images. Too often throughout history, the church has substituted pictures for the Real Presence. Then when God breaks into life from time to time, the church is found foolishly clinging to its inadequate images.

Why This Commandment Is Important

Such image making nonsense could be dismissed with a laugh were it not that certain dreadful consequences follow.

Image Making Depersonalizes God

Image making makes the great "I Am" into a thing. Why, you may wonder, would anyone want to do that? It keeps God in "His place." If God is a thing instead of a being, people can think about God, preach about God, study about God, write about God, prove God's existence, and use God to gratify their desires. That's a handy kind of god to have around—a cosmic bellhop to whom people give a 10 percent tip if he renders good service!

But God is not a thing. God is a person. And a person is satisfied only with loving relationships. Would you want your husband or wife or best friend to treat you the way that image makers treat God? Would you be flattered if they proved your existence, thought about you, talked about you, and studied you? A *person* you can know; a *thing* you can only know about. It is not enough merely to know that there is a God; do you know the God that you know is there? Can you say with the apostle Paul, "All I want is to know Christ and to experience the power of his resurrection . . ." (Philippians 3:10)?

Image Making Attempts to Control God

It's embarrassing to worship a god who neither conforms to our understanding nor does what we expect of God. Throughout history, we have tried to domesticate the Deity, to tame the Great Almighty. The efforts have always resulted in some form of idolatrous image. Every effort to comprehend God as an objective fact "out there" or an exalted ideal "in here" tries to take God into our possession. We do this by making idols, both metal and mental. Idolatry is not only the false image we hold in our hands but also the false idea we cherish in our hearts.

But God transcends everything we can grasp or contain. When we think we "have" God, the truth is that God has slipped through our grasp, and we are left clinging to some pitiful idol of our own making. We can never know God by seeking to grasp God, but only by allowing God to grasp us. We know God not by taking God into our possession, which is absurd and blasphemous, but by letting ourselves be possessed by God and by becoming open to God's infinite being, which is within us and around us and above us.

Image Making Destroys Human Personality and Freedom

An idolator creates a god like himself or herself, but with one exception: it lacks freedom and personality. Whether the idol is a rag doll from a savage tribe or some bloodless philosophical concept of a modern deist, it never acquires the personality and freedom of its maker. The image maker is more alive than his or her image. Thomas Carlyle observed that people become like the gods they serve. In gradually becoming like the gods he or she worships, an idolator ultimately loses freedom and personality. He or she becomes less a person and more a thing—a thing that cannot act but can only react to conditions around it.

The ancient psalmist said it best:

> Our God is in the heavens;
>   he does whatever he pleases.
> Their idols are silver and gold,
>   the work of men's hands.
> They have mouths, but do not speak;
>   eyes, but do not see.
> They have ears, but do not hear;
>   noses, but do not smell.
> They have hands, but do not feel;
>   feet, but do not walk;
>   and they do not make a sound in
>   their throat.
> *Those who make them are like them;*

so are all who trust in them
—Psalm 115:2-8, RSV (author's italics)

Worship of God, it turns out, is dangerous business. When it is distracted and distorted by vain images, it insults God by seeking to depersonalize and control God, and it dehumanizes the worshiper by destroying his or her personality and freedom. A person must worship the true God only in the right way.

Scripture References for Further Study

Image Making Consists of:

Worshiping the true God by a false image   *Exodus 32:4-6; Psalm 106:19-20; Hosea 8:5-6; 10:5*
Setting up idols in the heart   *Ezekiel 14:3-4*
Worshiping images   *Isaiah 44:17*
Sacrificing to images   *Psalm 106:37-38; Acts 7:41*

Image Making Changes:

The glory of God into an image   *Acts 17:29; Romans 1:23*
The truth of God into a lie   *Isaiah 44:20; Romans 1:25*

Those Who Practice Image Making:

Are vain in their imaginations   *Romans 1:21*
Are ridiculous   *Isaiah 41:7; 44:9-20*

Images Are Described as:

Local   *Deuteronomy 13:6; 1 Kings 20:23; 2 Kings 17:26*
Senseless   *Deuteronomy 4:28; Psalm 115:2-8*
Speechless   *Habakkuk 2:18; 1 Corinthians 12:2*
Helpless   *Isaiah 45:20; Jeremiah 10:5*
Unreal   *Jeremiah 5:7; 16:20; Galatians 4:8*
Nothing   *Isaiah 41:24; 1 Corinthians 8:4*

Images Are Worshiped with:

Feasts   *Exodus 32:5-6*
Sacrifices   *2 Kings 10:24; Jeremiah 48:35*
Libations   *Isaiah 57:6; Jeremiah 19:13*
Incense   *Jeremiah 19:13; 48:35, KJV*
Prayer   *1 Kings 18:26-29; Isaiah 44:17*

Singing and dancing *Exodus 32:19*
Bowing *1 Kings 19:18; 2 Kings 5:18, KJV*
Kissing *Hosea 13:2; Job 31:26-27*
Mutilation *1 Kings 18:28*
Child sacrifice *Deuteronomy 12:31; 2 Chronicles 33:6; Jeremiah 19:4-5; Ezekiel 16:20-21*

Images Are Worshiped in:

Temples *2 Kings 5:18; Hosea 8:14, KJV*
Altars *Exodus 34:13; Hosea 8:11*
Groves *Exodus 34:13, KJV; Isaiah 57:5; Jeremiah 2:20*
Homes *Judges 17:1-13; 2 Kings 23:12; Zephaniah 1:5*
Secret places *Isaiah 57:8, KJV; Ezekiel 8:7-12*

3

Do Not Misuse
God's Name

Turning to her daddy, seven-year-old Susie asked, "Why doesn't Tommy talk?"

"He can't," replied her father. "Babies as small as he is never talk."

"Oh yes, they do," Susie reassured him. "At Sunday church school last week our teacher told us that Job cursed the day he was born!"

Although Susie misunderstood the Scripture, she was not far from the truth. People learn bad language habits very early in life. Although some people think nothing of bad language, God takes what people say far more seriously than do the fading media censors. In fact, he devoted one of the Ten Commandments to this subject: "Do not use my name for evil purposes, because I, the LORD your God, will punish anyone who misuses my name."

What This Commandment Does Not Mean

Before considering the meaning of this commandment, it will help to clarify what it does not mean.

Obscenity

As much as I may dislike obscenity, that is not the target of the Third Commandment. Many people object to verbal sewage on the basis of aesthetics and social manners and not on the basis of holy Scripture. People abstain from using "dirty" words for the same reason they abstain from picking their nose in public and belching loudly at dinner. Social custom, not the Bible, says that four-letter Anglo-Saxon words are obscene and polysyllable Latin words are acceptable despite the fact that both may mean the same thing. I find some words personally offensive, but because they offend me, I do not necessarily conclude that they offend God. A violation of the cultural standards of good taste is not necessarily a violation of the law of God. Decency is not an attribute of God, C. S. Lewis reasons; therefore, many jokes lose their point in heaven.[1]

Words

The evil referred to in the Third Commandment lies not in a word itself but in the idea and intent behind it.

"That's what I like about you," the deacon said to the preacher. "When your golf ball goes into the rough, you don't swear like other people."

"That may be," the preacher confessed, "but where I spit, grass dies!"

Humorist Grady Nutt has suggested that somebody ought to invent cuss words for preachers. When a preacher hits his or her thumb with a hammer, he or she can say, "Verily, verily!" but that just doesn't get the pain out.

Joking aside, people under great stress express themselves in strong language. The words themselves, however, may not make any literal sense. Job complained, "Do you think that you can reprove words, when the speech of a despairing man is wind?" (Job 6:26, RSV). Most profanity is as empty of meaning as the wind. Consider the absurdity of persons who, on the one hand, loudly protest nuclear war but, on the other hand, daily consign others to the eternal fires of hell! More absurd, though less treacherous, is the fact that people damn the traffic light, their lost tools, and tears in their clothes.

The evil lies not in the words themselves but in the thought and intent behind them. People deceive themselves if they think that saying heck, gosh, gee whiz, darn, and dang keeps them from sinning when the thought and intent of their hearts may be the same as what lies behind the words' coarser counterparts. Can you imagine General Sherman saying "War is heck"?

The Third Commandment is not just a prudish caveat against offensive language but more like the warning posted on power plants: "Danger— High Voltage." When Uzzah accidentally touched the Ark of the Covenant, he was struck dead (2 Samuel 6:7). The word got around quickly: "Be careful how you touch God. You can get hurt!" Those ancient Jews understood what so many moderns miss: God is a real live wire. Take him seriously.

The Jews took the name of God so seriously that they refrained from speaking it at all. Even when reading the holy Scriptures, they substituted the word "Adonai," meaning "Lord," for the name written in the text. So universal was the practice that when vowels were added to the text, the vowels of "Adonai" were inserted in the consonants of the unspoken name of God. Thus, the word "Jehovah" is a hybrid word. It has the consonants of "Yahweh" (the unspoken name of God) and the vowels of "Adonai." This may be confusing. However, believe it or not, the ancient Jews reverenced God's name so much that they forgot how to pronounce it: the name "Yahweh" is a recent linguistic discovery.

Having considered what the Third Commandment does not mean, let us now give careful attention to what it does mean.

Misusing God's Name Means Not Taking God Seriously

People fail to take God seriously by swearing negligently which is breaking promises made in God's name, i.e., neglecting to do what they vowed to do. One of the most basic marks of moral maturity is the fidelity with which people keep their commitments. Some commitments, of course, are more important than others. If people can't do what they said they would do, then they have to make a choice. That requires a scale of priorities.

A Christian's commitment to Jesus Christ, obviously, ranks first in life. Coming next in order of importance are the vows he or she made in marriage. When one has given his or her word of honor to "love, honor and cherish, till death do us part," divorce is, at least, a violation of the Third Commandment. It is not the unforgivable sin, but let there be no mistake: divorce is a sin. Having given his or her word of honor, a Christian must not neglect to keep the promise.

Negligent swearing primarily concerns future affairs, but deceptive swearing concerns matters of past record. There may be some excuse for breaking a promise, but there is no excuse for lying about something that is already a known fact. People under oath who deliberately deceive others face a far more serious judgment in the hands of God than in the hands of any human court system.

Some people try to avoid negligent and deceptive swearing through evasive swearing. Jesus rebuked those in his day who believed that if

God's name was not specifically invoked, God would not be a partner
in the transaction. Jesus warned,

> "How terrible for you, blind guides! You teach, 'If someone swears by
> the Temple, he isn't bound by his vow; but if he swears by the gold in the
> Temple, he is bound.' . . . when [a person] swears by the Temple, he is
> swearing by it and by God, who lives there; and when someone swears by
> heaven, he is swearing by God's throne and by him who sits on it" (Mat-
> thew 23:16-22).

Jesus' point is clear: one can't keep God out of anything. Every
statement and promise and every human transaction is made in his presence and subject to his approval. Because a Christian is never released
from his or her solemn commitment to honesty, his or her simple yes or
no should require nothing more to verify it. Oaths are superfluous. Jesus
put it this way:

> "You have also heard that people were told in the past, 'Do not break
> your promise, but do what you have vowed to the Lord to do.' But now I
> tell you: do not use any vow when you make a promise. Do not swear by
> heaven, because it is God's throne; nor by earth, because it is the resting
> place for his feet; nor by Jerusalem, because it is the city of the great King.
> Do not even swear by your head, because you cannot make a single hair
> white or black. Just say 'Yes' or 'No'—anything else you say comes from
> the Evil One" (Matthew 5:33-37).

Oaths are a temporary concession to evil conditions and Jesus says
that they are completely unnecessary among Christians. But since Christians do not live in an ideal world, oaths are necessary in certain legal
situations. Jesus himself testified under oath at his trial (Matthew 26:63).
And even God took an oath. The author of Hebrews says, "When a
person makes a vow, he uses the name of someone greater than himself,
and the vow settles all arguments. To those who were to receive what
he promised God wanted to make it clear that he would never change
his purpose; so he *added his vow* to the promise" (Hebrews 6:16-17,
author's italics).

Because not everyone has a conscious awareness of God's involve-
ment with every word and deed, vows are commonly added to promises.
This is especially the case in the court system. "Do you swear to tell
the truth, the whole truth, and nothing but the truth, so help you God?"
the witness is asked. One witness who took the question seriously
responded, "If I *knew* the truth, the whole truth, and nothing but the
truth, I'd *be* God!"

With limited knowledge and weak resolution the Christian, nevertheless, knows that his or her entire life is a living oath subject to God's judgment and mercy. To take an oath adds nothing to the Christian's firm intention to tell the truth because the Christian knows that God will hold him or her accountable for every word and deed. Far from misusing God's name, he or she hallows it, not only in prayer but in all conversation and behavior.

Scripture References for Further Study

Misusing God's Name Consists of:

Swearing
> Negligent swearing   *Leviticus 19:12; Joshua 2:12, 17; 9:20; Deuteronomy 23:21; cf. Proverbs 25:19*
> Deceptive swearing   *Leviticus 19:12; Isaiah 48:1; Zechariah 8:17*
> Evasive swearing   *Matthew 5:33-37; 23:16-22*

Cursing
> Cursing God   *Leviticus 24:11, 16*
> Cursing humankind   *James 3:7-10*

Misusing God's Name Is Punished by:

Being cut off   *Zechariah 5:3-4, KJV*
Death   *Leviticus 24:16, 23; Psalm 59:12-13*
Curses rebounding to the one who curses   *Psalm 109:16-19*

Conditions for Swearing:

Permitted to those who forsake idols   *Jeremiah 4:1-2*
Limited to a simple yes or no   *Matthew 5:33-37; James 5:12*

Examples of Swearing:

Jesus' oath   *Matthew 26:63*
Paul's oath   *2 Corinthians 1:23; Galatians 1:20*
God's oath   *Hebrews 6:13-19*

Rewards of Those Who Love the Name of the Lord:

Isaiah 56:6-7

4

Don't Just Do Something. Stand There!

You gotta work before you play." This is one of the first lessons most people learn—or are supposed to learn early in life. Before one can ever express it in words, one knows there is a big difference between work and play. That difference is harder to define than many would suppose. It certainly has nothing to do with being paid for the activity. Many people get paid for playing, for doing things they would gladly do for nothing. And there are others, poor slaves, who are paid nothing for their drudgery.

One way to distinguish work from play is by defining "play" as "work one doesn't have to do." Why do it then? Because one wants to do it. And one wants to because the activity is in agreement with who one is and with one's interests, gifts, and talents. Work, on the other hand, is any activity that is in conflict with who one is. Regardless of one's interests, gifts, and talents, one has to do it.

Biblical Doctrine of Work

The Fourth Commandment makes clear that work was ordained by God. "Six days shalt thou labour, and do all thy work . . ." (Exodus 20:9, KJV). Long before God spoke to Moses on Mt. Sinai, however, God revealed to humankind the worth of work. In the second chapter of Genesis, before the first humans sinned, God commanded that Adam cultivate the Garden of Eden. Work, then, was not a penalty but an honorable activity.

Alan Richardson, in *The Biblical Doctrine of Work*, says, "Unlike the Greeks, who thought that working for one's living was beneath the dignity of a gentleman, the Hebrews looked upon daily toil as a normal part of the divine ordering of the world, and no man was exempt from it."[1] The writer of First Samuel sees no reason to hide the fact that King Saul was a common laborer (1 Samuel 11:5). The title "servant of the Lord" was a prestigious title (Genesis 26:24; Exodus 14:31).

Although work was ordained by God as an honorable activity, it soon became corrupted by sin. One of the consequences of humankind's fall into sin was that humankind has to work instead of doing what it wishes.

"Because of what you have done, the ground will be under a curse. You will have to work hard all your life to make it produce enough food for you. It will produce weeds and thorns, and you will have to eat wild plants. You will have to work hard and sweat to make the soil produce anything . . ." (Genesis 3:17-19).

Some might assume from this passage that the difference made by the curse of sin is in the amount of exertion humankind had to put forth. Yet it is hardly reasonable to suppose that Adam's muscles before the fall into sin were flabby from disuse. Rather, the difference is more likely to be that before he sinned, what he did was in agreement with who he was, i.e., play. After he sinned, what he did was in conflict with who he was, i.e., his work became toilsome and compulsive. Before sin, perhaps Adam approached his work like an enthusiastic pheasant hunter who eagerly arises at dawn for a day of hunting and returns home sweaty, happy, and exhausted at the end of the day. But after he sinned, his work became the daily grind of the thistle puller who forces himself from his bed utterly contrary to his inner nature.

Work ultimately becomes not only irksome but also compulsive. It gives dreary structure to an otherwise meaningless life. During the 1982 recession, Diane Sawyer reported on the CBS morning news that for every 1 percent rise in unemployment, there is a 4 percent rise in the suicide rate. A person's very survival depends on doing things one would rather not do. No wonder there is so much dissatisfaction and unhappiness in this world!

Biblical Doctrine of Play

Whether an activity is work or play depends not on what one does but on one's attitude. A fisherman's work can be the gardener's play and vice versa. Work is anything one does when one would rather be doing something else. Play is the "something else." It flows spontaneously from the kind of person one is.

Play is an important part of worship. Moses' sister Miriam led the women of Israel in a celebrative dance after Israel's miraculous deliverance from Egypt at the Red Sea (Exodus 15:20). When the Ark of the Covenant was brought into Jerusalem, the Scriptures tell us that David "danced with all his might to honor the LORD" (2 Samuel 6:14). In its highest form worship can't be spoken. When words fail, people sing and dance to express worship. Even the weeping prophet Jeremiah pictured the new age as one of play: "You shall adorn yourself with timbrels, and shall go forth in the dance of the merrymakers" (Jeremiah 31:4, RSV).

Worship that is contrived labor is not worship but sacrilege. True worship, like play, flows from one's heart. Jesus said, " 'Whoever believes in me, streams of life-giving water will pour out from his heart' " (John 7:38).

The Biblical Doctrine of Sabbath

The Fourth Commandment says, "Observe the Sabbath and keep it holy . . . the seventh day is a day of rest dedicated to me. On that day no one is to work . . ." (Exodus 20:8-10). To our compulsive generation the Lord, in effect, says, "Don't just do something. Stand there! Stand there regularly enough and long enough to discover and reaffirm who you are in relation to your Creator."

It is an important commandment. Although the sabbath is only one-seventh as long as the work week, it is the only day that God blessed and hallowed. This implies that humankind's chief end is not labor but, rather, rest and worship. Jesus picked up this theme in the home of Mary and Martha when he commended Mary for choosing the "right thing," that is, enjoying him rather than laboring in the kitchen with her sister (Luke 10:38-42).

There are three considerations involved in truly restful rest. Rest is not necessarily inactivity. In modern times much work is not physically demanding and, consequently, does not require physical rest. Rest is something that contrasts pleasantly with what one does most of the time. Rest is something one does because one enjoys the activity itself, not just the results. Golf becomes work if the only thing about it that interests the golfer is lowering his or her score.

The writer of Hebrews describes Christian life as a perpetual sabbath rest. He begins by quoting Genesis, "God rested on the seventh day from all his work" (Hebrews 4:4). He reminds his readers, "Those who first heard the Good News did not receive that rest, because they did not believe" (Hebrews 4:6). Then he argues "There are, then, others who are allowed to receive it . . . there still remains for God's people a rest like God's resting on the seventh day" (Hebrews 4:6-9). Finally he concludes, "Let us, then, do our best to receive that rest, so that no one of us will fail as they did because of their lack of faith" (Hebrews 4:11). In none of these references does the sabbath mean a calendar day, nor does rest mean mere inactivity.

> Rest is not quitting
> The busy career;
> Rest is the fitting
> Of self to its sphere.
> 'Tis loving and serving
> The highest and best!
> 'Tis onwards, unswerving,
> And that is true rest.[2]

The sabbath is not just a day but a life-style. Creation contains built-in rhythms. Just as the timing of its parts must be right for an engine to run smoothly, so there are timings that must be observed if humankind and the universe are to run as they ought. The fundamental cycle that God built into things alternates between doing and being, work and rest. The Fourth Commandment says that even animals need and deserve rest (Exodus 20:10).

The sabbath was originally the seventh day of the week, Saturday. But it was changed by the early church to the first day of the week, Sunday. This significant change did not come about through any specific command but through spiritual circumstances. Sunday was the day on which Christ arose to begin a new creation. Until he arose, believers worked *toward* the sabbath. After he arose, believers worked *from* the sabbath. The faith-rest life of the Christian is the beginning point, not the end. Consequently, sabbath was celebrated on Sunday instead of Saturday.

To neglect the sabbath makes living a task, a job, work. God doesn't need a holy day; people do. "The Sabbath was made for the good of man . . ." Jesus said (Mark 2:27). He "went about doing good . . ." (Acts 10:38, KJV). But people just go about. They must learn to stop in order to let their souls catch up with their bodies. "We mustn't confuse business for blessedness; activity must not pass for spirituality. What we are is more important than what we do."[3] In filling their lives with endless activity, people often empty them of meaning.

We may joke about the strict sabbath rules of Pilgrims and Puritans, but the joke is on us. They did not live in such an age of unrest like ours. They were not as vexed as we with mental illness, alcoholism, nervous breakdowns, and suicide. We are the most entertained and least happy people on earth. The fact is that we can't break the sabbath; we can only be broken upon it.

To observe the sabbath is to make living play. Remembering that we are children of God pushes the boundaries of life infinitely beyond the dull, monotonous routine of toil and transforms it. Two brick layers were asked, "What are you doing?" The first said, "Laying bricks." The second answered, "I'm building a cathedral." For some people life is laying just one brick after another—a lot of work! But for others life is cathedral building, i.e., play. Before one can build a cathedral, one has to know who one is and what one's place is in life's master plan. And the Sabbath is the time when one discovers these things.

Years ago, an NBC radio announcer received a letter from an old sheepherder in Idaho. "I enjoy your programs," he wrote, "but I want to ask a favor of you. It is rather lonely up here in the hills, and I have not much to amuse me except my radio. I used to play my violin, but it has gotten badly out of tune. Would you be so kind to pause on your next program to strike "A" so that I could tune my violin and enjoy its music again?"

Is your life out of tune with God? How long has it been since you heard "A"? Don't just do something. Stand there until you hear "A." Then retune your life to play in harmony with God's great cosmic chorus.

SCRIPTURES FOR FURTHER STUDY

Christ's Use of the Sabbath:

He observed the Sabbath   *Luke 4:16*
He taught on the Sabbath   *Luke 4:31; 6:6*
He healed on the Sabbath   *Luke 6:6-11; 13:10-17; 14:1-6; John 5:1-18*
He is Lord of the Sabbath   *Mark 2:28*

The Sabbath Is Observed by:

Not working   *Exodus 20:10; Leviticus 23:3; Deuteronomy 5:14*
Not buying or selling   *Nehemiah 10:31; 13:15-17*
Not carrying burdens   *Nehemiah 13:15, 19; Jeremiah 17:21-22*
Worshiping   *Ezekiel 46:3; Acts 16:13*
Reading Scripture   *Acts 13:27; 15:21*

Preaching   *Acts 13:14-15, 44; 17:2-3; 18:4*
Deeds of mercy   *Matthew 12:12; Luke 13:10-16; John 9:14*
Deeds of necessity   *Matthew 12:1; Luke 13:15; 14:1-5*

The Sabbath Is Observed on the:

Seventh day by Jews   *Exodus 20:9-11*
First day by Christians   *John 20:19; Acts 20:7; 1 Corinthians 16:2*

Disobedience Punished by:

National destruction   *Nehemiah 13:15-18; Jeremiah 17:27*
Death of the offender   *Exodus 31:12-15; Numbers 15:32-36*

Obedience Rewarded by:

Joy and honor   *Isaiah 58:13-14*
Divine blessing   *Isaiah 56:2*
Human benefit   *Mark 2:27*

The Sabbath Is a Sign of:

God's covenant with his people   *Exodus 31:13, 17*
People's faith-rest in God   *Hebrews 4:5-11*

5

Honor—Parental and Otherwise

The Bible says that the Ten Commandments were written on two tablets of stone (Exodus 24:12; 34:1). What it does not tell is how these Ten Commandments were arranged on the tablets. That there were five on each tablet would be a natural assumption, but it is an unnatural division when the themes of the commandments are considered. From ancient times Biblical scholars have noticed that the first four commandments concern people's relationship with God and the last six concern people's relationship with people.

It may not matter very much how the commandments were arranged on stone tablets, but it is important to note the dual themes. Judaism was the first world religion to combine worship (relationship with God) with ethical behavior (relationship with humankind). The gods of Mt. Olympus neither were ethical in their own behavior nor made ethical demands of their worshipers. In biblical religion, however, Yahweh is the Law-Giver. Ethics is theology at work; the Ten Commandments are the *Shema* in overalls.

Considered thematically, the commandments do not divide into two equal parts, five and five, but into two parts of four and six. The Fifth Commandment begins the second "table of the law": people's responsibility toward their neighbors. In this section God orders people to become more human by controlling certain physical desires humans share with animals. God calls people to something better. What inclination needs control in the Fifth Commandment? It is instinctive for most animals to care for their young, but no species of animal cares for its old. God makes it clear, however, that he expects children to provide for their parents in need as much as he expects parents to provide for their children in need. "Honor your father and your mother," he declares.

Our modern age does not give the elderly the place of honor they had in earlier times and so richly deserve. Nearly everyone, from Madison Avenue to the local church, honors youth. Although that's a good idea, young age is not the age on which the Bible puts the emphasis. Moses said, "Show respect for old people and honor them" (Leviticus 19:32). And Peter added, ". . . You younger men must submit yourselves to the older men" (1 Peter 5:5).

A youth-centered culture is a backward-facing culture. It is a society in which people honor what they used to be instead of what they are going to be.

Honor Your Father and Mother—the Primary Reference

This Fifth Commandment is addressed primarily to adults. It is not a biblical billy club with which frustrated parents can beat their rebellious children into submission. Parents who try to get respect from their children by quoting this Scripture passage will be as successful as if they were to steer their car by honking the horn. The Fifth Commandment has more to do with medical care, old-age pensions, and retirement homes than with disobedient minors. It means quite simply when parents have to depend on their children, the children should not let them down. Honor your father and mother.

Although Social Security, Medicare, and old-age pensions have largely taken over the kind of responsibilities enjoined by this commandment, no *system* can honor a father and mother for children. Many systems are terribly impersonal and even insultingly dehumanizing. When parents are no longer productive members of society, they need more than ever to be honored and reassured of their worth.

Honor Everyone—the Secondary Reference

The Fifth Commandment doesn't limit honor to one's parents. The apostle Peter said, "Respect everyone" (1 Peter 2:17). "Honor your father and mother" is the *beginning,* not the end of basic Christian behavior. Not only should children honor their parents, but parents should honor their children. Whites should honor blacks, and blacks should honor whites. The rich should honor the poor, and the poor should honor the rich. The weak should honor the strong, and the strong should honor the weak.

Jesus gave this command its highest application when he declared that whatever one does to the "least important of these brothers of mine," one does to him (Matthew 25:40). If one would honor Jesus Christ, one will honor not only his or her parents but every living soul.

Honor takes many different forms. It is much more than sending greeting cards and giving flowers on Mother's Day. The way in which parents honor their children, for instance, differs from the way children honor their parents. It is a dishonor to treat everyone alike without respect to differing needs and responsibilities. True honor takes into account the age and situation of the people involved and the nature of the relationship.

One of the reasons the generation gap is such a problem is that it is not wide enough. Too many adults try to act as though they were teenagers, and too many teenagers try to act as though they were adults. When all of the actors are trying to read the lines of someone else, it is no wonder that the play gets all fouled up. A child cannot honor his or her parents while refusing to accept the role of a dependent. And parents cannot honor their children while evading their parental responsibilities.

To make matters more complicated, the roles keep changing. For parents, giving true honor takes into account the growing competency, responsibility, and independence of children. For children, honor has many expressions. To a small child, it means obedience to parents. To an adolescent, it means respect for parents. To an adult child it means kindness, thoughtfulness, and care of parents. A boy will never become a man and a girl will never become a woman if he or she must always *obey* his or her parents, but children never outgrow the duty to honor their parents. The time may come when parents must obey the children. But even then, and especially then, the child must find ways to honor the parents, to affirm their dignity and worth.

The apostle Paul reminds people that the Fifth Commandment is the first commandment with a promise: ". . . so that all may go well with you, and you may live a long time in the land" (Ephesians 6:3). It would be a mistake to interpret that as guaranteeing extra years of life for the individual who honors his or her parents. In the biblical context the promise applies more to the nation and society than to individuals. The commandments were given before Israel entered and occupied the Promised Land. They were rules that preserved the social order. Good individuals may die young, but people in those cultures in which people are good to one another tend to live to a ripe old age. "[That] you may live a long time in the land" is not a tempting bribe to good conduct, but a statement of fact about nations and tribes in which honor is found.

Remember, the Bible doesn't tell who is to honor one, but whom one is to honor—one's parents and everyone else. One obeys the Fifth Commandment, not by demanding that others honor oneself but by taking the initiative to honor others.

Scripture References for Further Study

Examples of Dishonoring Parents:

Striking one's parents   *Exodus 21:15*
Cursing one's parents   *Exodus 21:17; Proverbs 20:20; 30:11*
Stealing from one's parents   *Proverbs 28:24*
Ridiculing one's parents   *Proverbs 30:17*
Refusing to help one's parents   *Matthew 15:3-9*

Examples of Honoring Parents:

Obeying one's parents   *Proverbs 6:20; Ephesians 6:1; Colossians 3:20*
Honoring the elderly   *Leviticus 19:32; 1 Peter 5:5*
Paying attention to parents' teaching   *Proverbs 1:8-9; 15:5; 23:22*
Showing appreciation   *Proverbs 23:22*
Making one's parents proud   *Proverbs 23:25*
Honoring heavenly Father   *Malachi 1:6; Hebrews 12:9*

One Who Breaks This Commandment Is:

Punished by death   *Exodus 21:15, 17; Deuteronomy 21:18-21; Matthew 15:4*

One Who Observes This Commandment Is:

Rewarded by life   *Ephesians 6:2-3*

6

Miscellaneous Murder

Now we come to the most controversial commandment of all. Asked to name the Ten Commandments, most people would begin the list with "Thou shalt not kill," for it names the most obvious evil that God has prohibited. Obvious though the commandment's injunction may be to all cultures—biblical and otherwise—people today are not at all agreed on its scope and intention.

The Sixth Commandment is not a blanket interdiction against killing but, rather, a specific prohibition of murder, the intentional taking of another person's life. Old Testament history makes clear that the ancient Hebrews didn't understand this commandment as outlawing either war or capital punishment but only personal blood vengeance. In this limited sense it is the least troublesome of the Ten Commandments. "Thou shalt not murder" bothers most of us about as much as if God had commanded, "Thou shalt not spit on the moon." We have never murdered anyone and don't intend to. Adultery, stealing, and lying . . . ah, they are different matters! But more about them later.

Many people, when asked if they approve of sex and violence, would answer, "Yes and no!" In spite of all the violence in our world, few people approve of it. Only one person in one thousand has actually broken the Sixth Commandment in its narrow sense of murder. And many murderers are psychopaths incapable of feeling normal guilt for their bad behavior. So for murderers and nonmurderers alike, the Sixth Commandment is the least troublesome of the ten.

As long as one sticks to the primary reference of the Sixth Commandment, one is on safe, noncontroversial ground. But one doesn't need to buy a book to find out that God doesn't approve of killing people. We therefore leave the safe garrison of the obvious to explore the deep forests and dark caves that surround this commandment. Before we set forth on our journey, I warn you that there are snipers lurking in the darkness along the way ready to attack if we trespass their codes of behavior. I will try to be a reliable guide, but I confess that other guides, whose wisdom and Christian commitment I highly respect, would take you a different route.

Miscellaneous Murder

The primary reference of the Sixth Commandment is murder, the taking of a human life, which is as sacred as the breath of God that gave it (Genesis 2:7). But there are other ways of terminating life besides "murder most foul." Let us consider some miscellaneous acts that violate the sanctity of life in different ways.

Suicide

All of life is sacred, including one's own. One chooses neither the time and circumstances of birth nor the time and circumstances of death. Those matters belong exclusively to the Creator. "You do not belong to yourselves, but to God" (1 Corinthians 6:19). To take one's life, therefore, destroys what belongs to God and, furthermore, deprives others of the love and service one could have devoted to them. Suicide is a violation of the Sixth Commandment. There are other ways of shortening life that may be less violent but are just as effective.

Drugs, Alcohol, Cigarettes, and Gluttony

Alcohol is our nation's number-one killer drug. It kills far more people than heroin and cocaine. Fifty percent of all fatal car accidents involve drinking drivers. If there had been drunken drivers in Moses' day, there would probably have been eleven commandments. Alcoholism not only kills people dead; it kills them alive, which is worse! Nine million alcoholics[1] suffer a living hell in the United States. They are breaking the Sixth Commandment by killing themselves and others.

So severe is the problem of alcoholism in our day that many Christians advocate total abstinence as the only responsible position. The Bible clearly commands temperance (1 Timothy 3:8; Titus 2:3) and condemns drunkenness (Proverbs 23:29-35; 1 Corinthians 6:9-10; Ephesians 5:18), but it does not insist on total abstinence. Jesus himself miraculously changed water into wine and was widely known as a wine drinker (John

2:1-11; Matthew 11:19; Luke 7:34). Although total abstinence from all alcoholic beverages is not required behavior for Christians, it may be a necessary precaution for many whose environment or biology is conducive to drunkenness, a mortal sin.

Alcohol is not the only "nonviolent" killer. Cigarettes are a lethal substance, too. The U.S. Public Health Service estimates that one million children now in school will die of lung cancer before they reach the age of seventy. There is no doubt about it; cigarettes are killing people. Before an assassin broke the Sixth Commandment and took the life of Bobby Kennedy, the former Attorney General spoke of an assassin that breaks this commandment many times over.

At the present rate, one seventh of all Americans now alive—about 28 million people—will die prematurely of diseases associated with cigarette smoking. Every year cigarettes kill more Americans than were killed in World War I, the Korean War, and Vietnam combined. Each year cigarettes kill five times more Americans than traffic deaths do. The cigarette industry is peddling a deadly weapon. It is dealing in people's lives for financial gain.[2]

If this journey into the territory of miscellaneous acts of murder hasn't made you nervous yet, hang on to your hat. Around the corner there's another killer that looks like an old friend. Food is killing people in two ways: either people don't have enough of it or people have too much of it. Some of God's children die of starvation while others "dig" their own graves with their forks. They shorten their own lives by overeating and other people's lives by refusing to share the surplus of food. Those who indulge in drugs, alcohol, cigarettes, and gluttony commit suicide on the installment plan. It is a miscellaneous act of murder, a violation of the Sixth Commandment.

Abortion

Now we are in one of the most battle scarred territories of all. Recent controversy has polarized even the Christian community into two warring camps: prolife and prochoice. The problem is that both sides think they know more than they can possibly know. They have made up their minds about one of life's truly great enigmas: when does human life begin?

The prolifers, usually "big" on biology, believe that individual life begins at the moment of conception, pointing to the fact that the individual's unique genetic code is set the instant the sperm fertilizes the ovum. For this reason, they oppose abortion at any stage of pregnancy, even abortifacient contraception. They say that because a three-day-old embryo has a soul, it has the same right to life as the mother—even the right to eternal life. And furthermore, a woman with an IUD might have 250 children in heaven, all of whom were aborted before her fertilized ovum could be implanted in her uterus.

The prochoicers, on the other hand, believe just as passionately that individual life begins only at the moment of birth. Before birth the baby is considered as much a part of the mother's body as her appendix. They argue, therefore, that she has the right to do anything she wants with it and to take such action at any stage of pregnancy. This reasoning, however, leads them to approve the killing of premature babies whose lives could be saved with proper medical attention.

The point that I am making is that nobody knows for sure when an individual's life begins or, to put it in theological language, when ensoulment occurs. This mystery should make us humble, a virtue rarely found among argumentative combatants.

What does the Bible say about abortion? Not much. There is no direct statement in the New Testament and only one incidental reference to it in the Old Testament. Although the killing of an unborn child was not regarded as equivalent to murder by the Mosaic law, it was still considered a crime (Exodus 21:22-25). Christians today may differ in their political views concerning ways in which civil government should get involved in this issue, but all Christians should agree on the sanctity of life. Life is no accident. It is a divine gift. People dare not destroy what God has given.

Capital Punishment

Now we enter territory that has seen a lot of changes since Moses' day. Far from forbidding capital punishment, the Old Testament actually commands it for such crimes as adultery, sabbath breaking, and dishonoring parents (Leviticus 20:10; Numbers 15:32-36; Deuteronomy 21:18-21). Thank God that's not the law today, or you might not be able to read this unless it were printed on asbestos!

Yes, times have changed. The Old Testament contains laws that governed a primitive society. Those laws have been changed through the years by the gradual reduction of the number of crimes for which capital punishment is decreed. Are there any crimes in our modern age for which the death penalty is the proper punishment? Some Christians would say yes and others would say no. It seems to me that, like divorce and slavery, capital punishment is one of those infringements on the divine will that the Bible did not immediately eliminate. The underlying principle of the sanctity of human life leads us to respect all life, even the life of a murderer.

War

Again we plunge deeper into territory that has changed since Moses' day. On the one hand, those ancient Hebrews were told not to murder. On the other hand, they were commanded to wage "holy" wars against the heathen—not just any wars, mind you, but only those wars specifically decreed by God. Christians have disagreed among themselves through the centuries over the conditions under which one can conscientiously engage in war, and in our generation another great change has occurred in this territory. Our generation is the first generation that has in its power the ability to be the last generation. The experts are almost unanimous: global nuclear war would be global nuclear suicide. Consequently, nearly everyone seems to be in favor of nuclear disarmament. But the problem is that no nation wants to be the first to start disarmament. So nations go on madly stockpiling incredible arsenals of weapons that can kill both sides many times over.

To focus the issue more sharply, here's a puzzle for you. Two men are in a basement. A strong smell of gas is in the air. One has fifteen matches. The other has twenty matches. The question to answer is which one wins the game or is ahead of the other? If you can answer that question, you can answer the question of who is ahead in the nuclear arms race.

The nuclear arms race could destroy the human race. It seems clearer now than ever before that the only hope for this world's survival into the twenty-first century is for nations to trust God instead of armaments (Psalm 44:3-8; Zechariah 4:6).

Hate

We have come through many dangerous outposts in the territory surrounding the Sixth Commandment, but none is as "far out" as Jesus' command, "Love your enemies" (Matthew 5:44). John applies this saying directly to the Sixth Commandment, "Whoever hates his brother is a murderer . . ." (1 John 3:15). Now we are all caught. What started out as the least troublesome commandment has us in its grip.

Although we may never actually have killed anyone, let us confess that sometimes we have read the obituaries with pleasure. While the law of Moses restrains the end result of violence, the law of Jesus restrains the beginning cause of violence. He stops not only the hand that is about to strike but also the heart that is about to hate.

Nearly everyone has been guilty of some form of miscellaneous murder. That's bad news. But the good news is that God loves us and still has a wonderful plan for our lives. Moses, David, and Paul were all murderers whom God rescued and restored to great blessing and service. What God did for them, he can do for us. Our lives can save life, not destroy it.

Scripture References for Further Study
Kinds of Murder:

Voluntary homicide   *Exodus 21:14*
Involuntary homicide   *Numbers 35:9-15, 22-29*
Negligent homicide   *Exodus 21:28-30*
Conspiracy   *2 Samuel 12:9*
Political execution   *2 Chronicles 24:21-22*
Riot   *Proverbs 1:10-18*
Secret assassination   *Isaiah 26:21; Jeremiah 2:34*
Suicide   *1 Samuel 31:4-5; Matthew 27:5*

Victims of Murder:

Slaves   *Exodus 21:20-21*
Embryos   *Exodus 21:22-25*
Thieves   *Exodus 22:3*
Parents   *1 Timothy 1:9*
Prophets   *Jeremiah 26:15*

Murder Defiles:

Hands   *Isaiah 59:3, KJV*
Garments   *Lamentations 4:13-14*
Land   *Numbers 35:33; Psalm 106:38*

What God Does About Murder:

Abominates it   *Proverbs 6:16-17*
Curses it   *Genesis 4:11*
Avenges it   *Deuteronomy 32:43; 1 Kings 21:19; Hosea 1:4*

Punishment for Murder:

Cries out to heaven   *Genesis 4:10; Hebrews 12:24, KJV*
Life for life   *Genesis 9:5-6; Leviticus 24:21-22; Numbers 35:16-21; 30-34; Deuteronomy 19:11-13; Acts 28:4*

Murder Is Defined as Anger:

Matthew 5:21-22; 1 John 3:15

Our Search for Peace:

Commands about peace *Psalm 34:14; Ephesians 4:3; 6:14-15; Colossians 3:15; Romans 12:18*

Warnings about peace *Isaiah 48:22, KJV; Ezekiel 7:25, KJV; Luke 19:42*

Promises about peace *Psalm 29:11; 37:10-11, 37; 72:7, KJV; 119:165, KJV; Isaiah 26:3; 32:17-18; 65:25; Luke 1:78-79; 2:14; John 16:33; Acts 10:36; Ephesians 2:14-17; Colossians 1:20; 2 Thessalonians 3:16*

7

Vis-à-Vis Adultery

Jesus called the society in which he lived an "adulterous and sinful generation" (Mark 8:38, KJV). What words do you think he would use to describe ours?

Soap operas may not mirror what is happening in real life, but they do at least demonstrate what people in real life find to be entertaining. And entertainment reflects and is one of the factors that forms public attitudes. The University of Pennsylvania's Annenberg School of Communications reported the results of a 1981 survey of the sexual behavior portrayed in popular soap operas. Forty-nine percent of the intercourse suggested in the soaps was between unmarried lovers. Twenty-nine percent involved strangers, and six percent involved a married couple. "Given the growing viewership of these series and the audience composition," the report concluded, "soap operas are potentially a major force in the transmission of values and lifestyle and sexual information to youthful viewers." [1]

Ours is an adulterous and sinful generation. Even Christians are caught up in the moral climate; yet they are to be thermostats and not thermometers. They are supposed to change the environment and not merely reflect the attitudes of a decadent culture. The Christians' starting point is not the Gallup poll but the timeless Word of God, who declared on Mt. Sinai and throughout the Bible, "Do not commit adultery."

Adultery Adulterates

Why should people refrain from adultery? Because God said so! And he said so for several obvious reasons. First of all, adultery adulterates.

51

Sex is essentially pure. It is part of the creation that God pronounced good. But precisely because it is pure, it must be protected from adulteration. People need God's pure sex law for the same reason we need pure food and drug laws. The laws protect people from contaminants that would destroy health and happiness. The Bible is not against sex. To the contrary, it values sex enough to rescue it from adulteration.

Chapter 1 stated that often the good things in life are most easily turned into idols to which people give devotion that belongs only to God. The worship of Aphrodite, i.e. sexual sensation, diminishes rather than increases sexual pleasure. The Hollywood marriage-go-round is a public demonstration that sexual promiscuity kills marital happiness. The world isn't ready to return to strict Puritanism, but it cannot long survive the modern mudhole that makes sex a pastime, women mere playthings, and morality a joke.

Contrary to popular opinion, it is not the presence of love that makes sex chaste nor the absence of love that makes it sinful. The distinction between adultery and chastity does not depend upon one's state of feeling at the moment. The sex act, like other acts, is justified by far more definable criteria: by keeping promises, by charity, by obedience. When the criteria are met, the sexual union becomes total commitment.

Moses declared and Jesus confirmed that in the act of marriage, "the two will become one" (Genesis 2:24; Mark 10:8; cf. 1 Corinthians 6:16). Marriage is not just a union but a profound reunion. The point of the story about the woman being made from Adam's rib is that Adam's unity, which was divided in the creation of Eve, was restored in marriage. The marital reunion prefigures the soul's reunion with God and requires a level of self-surrender second only to surrender to God (Ephesians 5:28-33). When marital union is only partial, sex is hardly worth having at all—a momentary pleasure and a permanent loneliness.

There are many ways to adulterate sex. The Bible's pure sex law specifies a number of practices that are not safe and effective. On its list of forbidden practices are premarital intercourse (Deuteronomy 22:13-21; 1 Corinthians 6:9, KJV; 1 Thessalonians 4:1-8, KJV), extramarital intercourse (Proverbs 2:16-19; 5:15-22; 30:20), incest (Leviticus 18:6-18), sodomy (Leviticus 20:15-16), prostitution (Proverbs 6:24-33, KJV; 7:6-27), rape (Deuteronomy 22:25-29), and divorce (Mark 10:2-12). These are sexual practices that are so obviously destructive of the welfare of society and individuals that they are forbidden even by governments like the People's Republic of China, which has no belief in Moses or Jesus.

God does not bid and forbid just to be bossy. Out of compassion for people, God warns of the dangers of adulterated sex. People cannot improve their sex life by these forbidden practices. They will only destroy something precious.

God wants to set people free to enjoy sex to its fullest. One entire book in the Bible was written to celebrate the joys of romantic love. Do you suppose there is any significance in its initials? S.O.S.! In spite of all the modern books and information, people's love life is crying for help more now than ever before. Answering that plea are the Song of Solomon and the Ten Commandments. By defining the limits of sexual behavior, God protects sex from adulteration.

Adultery Fascinates

In the Sermon on the Mount, Jesus gave the ancient law of Moses a new depth of definition. "You have heard it was said, 'Do not commit adultery.' But now I tell you: anyone who looks at a woman and wants to possess her is guilty of committing adultery with her in his heart" (Matthew 5:27-28). Just as Jesus condemned not only murder but also the anger that causes it, so he condemned not only the act of adultery but also the mental fascination that motivates it.

So long has this generation suffered "sexploitation" that it has lost the ability to distinguish clearly between lust and love. Lechery is pictured on a wide screen with the playing of violins. People call it love, but it is not. The difference is found in the pronouns. Lust wants *it*, sex, the thing itself. Love wants *him* or *her*, the beloved. The *thing* is a sensory pleasure that occurs within one's own body. It is often said that a lustful man wants a woman. But that's not what he really wants. What he wants is pleasure for which a woman happens to be a convenient piece of apparatus. Lust is what makes one want sex even when one has no desire to be with the other. Love is what makes one want to be with the other even when one has no desire for sex.

Now to be perfectly honest, or 97 percent thereof, most people haven't come as far as Moses or as far as Jesus. Many have broken the Seventh Commandment in deed as well as thought. The important thing to note here is that God looks upon all as sinners. Jesus says to self-righteous prudes, "Before you condemn the adulterer, look to your own heart." If thoughts could be read, faces would be redder!

The secular press had a lot of laughs a few years ago about President Carter's confession that he had committed adultery in his heart. The fact was, of course, that he spoke the truth, not only about himself but also about all of us. The only difference was that President Carter was human enough to admit it. Are we?

Since we are all adulterers in thought, if not also in deed, what then shall we do about it? Jesus offers some very practical advice in strong metaphorical terms:

> "If your right eye causes you to sin, take it out and throw it away! It is much better for you to lose a part of your body than to have your whole body thrown into hell. If your right hand causes you to sin, cut it off and throw it away! It is much better for you to lose one of your limbs than to have your whole body go off to hell" (Matthew 5:29-30).

Jesus' advice is meant to be taken seriously but not literally. Most people can see as much with the left eye as with the right and do as much with the left hand as with the right. The sin is not found in the eye or hand but in the heart. Jesus and good sense demand that people eliminate anything that causes them to stumble.

Jesus' principle does not impose a uniform code of behavior on everyone. What causes one person to sin may not cause another to sin. In December 1975 Israel's chief rabbi, Ovadiah Yosef, declared that Orthodox Jewish men could listen to a woman singing on the radio but only if they did not know her personally. "According to some religious authorities, a woman's voice can turn one's thoughts away from the spiritual. . . . But if a man has never met the singer, there is little danger of his being seduced."[2] *No arguments about that!* But don't laugh so hard that you lose the point. Few Christians would go to such extremes to avoid an adulterous relationship, but all Christians need to know their limits. Every Christian is responsible for himself or herself. If something causes you to sin, get rid of it. But remember this is do-it-yourself surgery. Nobody has the right to amputate a brother's or sister's hand or eye.

Late one night a pastor got a phone call from one of his parishioners who asked, "Will God forgive a person for committing adultery?" The pastor's answer was, "That depends. Did you, or are you about to?"

Adultery in act or thought is a sin which no child of God would deliberately commit, but it is not the unpardonable sin. King David, the Samaritan woman, and the woman taken in the act of adultery broke the Seventh Commandment but were forgiven and restored to holy living. No matter what one has done, no matter how guilty one feels, one can confess it right now and hear Jesus say, "Neither do I condemn thee: go, and sin no more" (John 8:11, KJV). One can start all over again with a sex life that is as pure and unadulterated as Jesus himself.

Scripture References for Further Study

Forbidden Sexual Practices:

Premarital intercourse   *Deuteronomy 22:13-21; 1 Corinthians 6:9-18, KJV; 1 Thessalonians 4:1-8, KJV*

Extramarital intercourse   *Leviticus 18:20; 2 Samuel 11:2-4, 27; Proverbs 2:16-19; 5:15-22; 6:20-35; 30:20; Romans 7:2-3; Hebrews 13:4*

Incest   *Leviticus 18:6-18; 20:10-12, 14, 17, 19-21; 1 Corinthians 5:1-5*

Sodomy   *Leviticus 18:22; 20:13; Romans 1:26-32*

Bestiality   *Leviticus 18:23; 20:15-16*

Prostitution   *Proverbs 6:24-33; 7:6-27; Jeremiah 5:7-9*

Rape   *Deuteronomy 22:25-29*

Divorce   *Mark 10:2-12*

Lust   *Matthew 5:27-30*

Laws Related to Adultery:

Trial by ordeal   *Numbers 5:11-30*

Grounds for divorce   *Matthew 5:32; 19:9*

Adultery Is Punished by:

Death   *Leviticus 20:10; Deuteronomy 22:22-24; Job 31:9-12; John 8:5*

Damnation   *1 Corinthians 6:9-10; Galatians 5:19-21; Revelation 21:8*

Forgiveness Was Granted to:

David   *Psalm 32; Psalm 51*

Samaritan woman   *John 4:5-42*

Woman taken in the act   *John 8:3-11*

8

You Tell Others Not
to Steal—Do *You* Steal?

During the refuse workers' strike in New York City a few years ago, one desperate householder found a clever way to get rid of his garbage. He gift wrapped it and left it on the seat of his unlocked car. By evening it was gone.

It should be easy to cry out against stealing. After all, even robbers object to being robbed. "Thou shalt not steal" appears to be so self-evident that God seems to be wasting breath by giving the Eighth Commandment. If he hadn't said it, we would be telling ourselves, "Thou shalt not steal." Everybody, religious and nonreligious alike, agrees that stealing is wrong.

The apostle Paul writes, "You tell others not to steal—do *you* steal?" (Romans 2:21, *Living Bible*). His question forces one to look at stealing from a different perspective. The Bible does not allow one to be the complainant but, rather, forces one to be the defendant before the bar of justice. God's Word forces one to reexamine one's basic convictions about people and property.

Conviction

Of course, times are different now. Changes since Moses' day have made things easier for the guilty conscience. The shift from a simple farming culture to a complex industrial society has given many thieves a guilt-proof excuse: "After all," they say, "I'm not hurting anyone in particular." One who would never think of stealing a neighbor's rake may steal with impunity from corporations, insurance companies, or governments.

The thief has been given a convenient excuse not only by changes in society but by changes in himself or herself. He or she has changed from a guilt ethic (restraint by conscience) to a shame ethic (restraint by fear of apprehension). "Thou shalt not get caught" is widely regarded as the Eleventh Commandment.

The successful criminal receives admiration and approval. Our society rewards bigness and success. If one kills a person, one is a murderer; if one kills twenty-five persons, one is a psychopath; if one kills a million persons, one is a national hero. If a person steals a thousand dollars, society sends him or her to prison; but if one steals a million dollars, society sends that person to Congress! Many philanthropists give away when they ought to be giving back.

People have found respectable ways to break the Eighth Commandment. A full-page advertisement in a popular magazine offers to sell a book entitled "How to Legally Steal Yourself Rich." There are so many legal ways to "steal" that it is a wonder that anyone resorts to crime. The Bible condemns the dishonest rich more than the desperate poor for stealing. "People don't despise a thief if he steals food when he is hungry . . ." (Proverbs 6:30). But the prophet Micah thundered,

> "Listen, you people who assemble in the city! In the houses of evil men are treasures which they got dishonestly. They use false measures, a thing I hate. How can I forgive men who use false scales and weights? Your rich men exploit the poor, and all of you are liars. So I have already begun your ruin and destruction because of your sins" (Micah 6:9-13).

Jesus sternly warned the scribes who "take advantage of widows and rob them of their homes, and then make a show of saying long prayers. Their punishment," he declares, "will be all the worse!" (Mark 12:40). At the close of his life he drove out "respectable" moneychangers from the temple, saying they had made it a "den of thieves" (Matthew 21:13, KJV), but, on the other hand, he welcomed the repentant thief into paradise. They were all thieves, but what a difference in the way the Savior regarded them! What kind of thief are you?

Convention

The kind of thieves that Jesus considered most reprehensible were those who did not live by their convictions but by conventions. Business fraud is conventional thievery. When asked about his standard of business ethics, one man gave this example: "If someone buys a tie for ten dollars but mistakenly gives me a hundred dollar bill for it, business ethics is whether or not I should tell my partner."

Excessive profits and professional fees become theft when they take more than is fair of another person's goods. There comes a point when profits are not just obscene; they constitute outright stealing.

Unlimited profits have been justified by the so-called "trickle-down" theory. This theory holds that the poor are better off if, instead of giving money to them, money is given to the rich who will then let it trickle down to the poor workers. The actual result of this theory can be seen all over Latin America, where most countries are ruled by a small handful of multi-millionaire politicians, landowners, and industrialists while the rest of the people suffer grinding poverty. There is no justification for excessive profits and professional fees. It is theft.

Withholding a laborer's just wage is another form of business fraud (Deuteronomy 24:14-15; James 5:4). Honesty demands of the employer a fair day's wage for a fair day's work and of the employee a fair day's work for a fair day's wage. Giving thirty hours' pay for forty hours of work and taking forty hours' pay for thirty hours of work are both stealing.

Another kind of conventional thievery is found in the common failure of people to pay debts. Christians, of course, must have compassion on poor people who can't pay their bills (Matthew 18:21-35). Yet anyone who carelessly spends more than one earns for anything other than bare necessities is a thief.

Bribery is another form of conventional theft. When a lobbyist offered to give a new sports car to a politician in exchange for his vote, the politician indignantly declined, saying it was illegal and immoral to sell his vote. "Well, then," the lobbyist said, "suppose I *sell* you the car for ten dollars?"

"In that case," the politician replied, "I'll take two of them!"

Conventional standards suggest that a politician is honest if when he or she is "bought," he or she stays "bought." Woe be unto the one who fails to vote the way his or her election campaign contributors demand.

Bribery reaches not only to high political office but also to the lowly church office. Mail comes across my desk saying, "Pick any gift. It's free with your order." I am offered transistor radios, warming trays, and lamps if I buy the church's mimeograph stencils and plastic binders from certain suppliers. But to spend the church's money in ways that benefit me personally is stealing.

Nations as well as individuals can break the Eighth Commandment. International exploitation is another form of conventional theft. Columbus, for example, didn't discover America. Columbus *found* America. And when he found it, it already had an owner. Columbus had no more right to claim it for Spain than I have to "discover" another person's car and claim it for myself.

Part of America's immense wealth was gained at the expense of weaker economies, not only in colonial times but even today. We mine and import huge quantities of raw materials from Third World under-developed nations. But since our tariff laws prevent these nations from exporting finished goods to us, they cannot develop their own industries. Therefore, they must buy their own raw materials back from us in refined, processed, or finished form at a profit to American industry. Thus, the rich get richer and the poor get poorer. Yet it is stealing. The "slickest" theft of all is getting someone else to do your stealing for you.

Finally, even money itself becomes a swindle. Inflation steals the value of money from everybody's pocket.

"You tell others not to steal—do *you* steal?" That's the disturbing question that convicts us all of our conventional thievery.

Conversion

What are we going to do about stealing? First of all, let us consider the sinfulness of theft. Jesus said, "From [the] heart come the evil ideas which lead [people] . . . to rob . . ." (Matthew 15:19). All theft, legal or illegal, involves the same unclean thinking: contempt for other people.

We are all God's guests on earth. To presume on his hospitality by regarding his creation as ours unconditionally is theft. The apostle Paul not only demands that the thief quit stealing but also commands the thief to go to work so that he or she may start giving. Every nongiver robs somebody of something. The prophet Malachi pictures people who probably wouldn't have pilfered a penny from a piggy bank as cosmic bandits robbing the bank of heaven! "Ye have robbed me," says the Lord, ". . . In tithes and offerings. . . . ye have robbed me, even this whole nation" (Malachi 3:8-9, KJV).

Salvation from theft begins with repentance and restitution. Zacchaeus provides the model. He said, "'I will give half my belongings to the poor, and if I have cheated anyone, I will pay him back four times as much.' Jesus said to him, 'Salvation has come to this house today . . .'" (Luke 19:8-9).

The good news is that God loves thieves so much that Jesus died for them. Through his atonement they can be forgiven. Jesus died between two thieves to save all thieves.

> The dying thief rejoiced to see
> that fountain in his day;
> And there may I, though vile as he,
> Wash all my sins away . . .[1]

Scripture References for Further Study

Kinds of Theft:

Extortion   *Luke 3:12-13*
Bribery   *Exodus 23:8; Isaiah 1:23; Micah 7:3-4; Matthew 26:15*
Business fraud   *Leviticus 19:35-36; Deuteronomy 25:13-14; Proverbs 11:1; Amos 8:4-6; Micah 6:9-12*
Looting   *Proverbs 1:13; Ezekiel 39:10*
Deprivation of the poor   *Proverbs 22:22; Mark 12:38-40*
Using stolen goods   *Amos 3:10-11*

Property Stolen:

Money   *Proverbs 30:7-9; John 12:6*
People   *Exodus 21:16; Deuteronomy 24:7*
Wages   *Leviticus 19:13; Deuteronomy 24:14-15; James 5:4*
Food   *Proverbs 6:30-31*
Loyalty   *2 Samuel 15:6*
Tithes   *Malachi 3:8, 9*

Causes of Theft:

Unclean thinking   *Matthew 15:19-20; Mark 7:21-22*
Attraction of what is forbidden   *Proverbs 9:17; Romans 7:7*

Punishment for Theft:

Cursed   *Zechariah 5:1-4*
Shut out of the kingdom of God   *1 Corinthians 6:9-10*
Restitution   *Exodus 22:1-5; Leviticus 6:1-7; Ezekiel 33:15; Luke 19:1-9*

9

The Sevenfold Abomination

Although the primary reference of the Ninth Commandment is to formal testimony before a court of law, the commandment illustrates the principle of honesty that applies to all of life. Slander loudly proclaimed before a judge or quietly whispered to a neighbor differs only in that the former has the extra guilt of a broken oath. I have never been called upon to give testimony at a trial, but the Ninth Commandment still speaks to me in a far more personal way: "Tell the truth."

Lying is a sevenfold abomination. Ancient Hebrew wisdom declares,

There are seven things that the Lord hates and cannot tolerate:
A proud look,
  a lying tongue,
  hands that kill innocent people,
  a mind that thinks up wicked plans,
  feet that hurry off to do evil,
  a witness who tells one lie after another,
  and a man who stirs up trouble among friends.
                      —Proverbs 6:16-19

All seven of these vices are found in the person who breaks the Ninth Commandment. Every part of him or her—tongue, hands, mind, and feet— is infected with the disease of dishonesty. Not only does God find such people intolerable, but nobody else can stand them either.

Tell the Truth

"Love covers a multitude of sins," so the Bible affirms (1 Peter 4:8, RSV). But it is much more common to find people acting as though it said, "Lying covers a multitude of sins." For, of course, lying does—temporarily! People lie to avoid the consequences of something else that they've done wrong.

It is easy to tell one lie but hard to tell only one. A person can't eat just *one* potato chip, and a person can't tell just *one* lie. One lie leads to another and another and another until one is caught in a tangled web of dishonesty. And those who start out to tell white lies soon become color blind.

"A lie is an abomination unto the Lord . . . and an ever present help in time of trouble." This statement is a mismatch of Bible passages but a true reflection of life. When people get into trouble, a lie always looks more like an asset than a liability. But clinging to it in self-defense is like holding onto a lightning rod in a thunderstorm.

As with individuals, so with governments: the more deeply they get into trouble, the more apt they are to seek an escape through lying. Truth is the first casualty in every war. Governments consider it their patriotic duty to deceive the enemy and, incidentally, their own people. Thus, each government inflates the battlefield losses of the other and deflates its own. "National security" becomes the handy detergent with which a government washes the black out of every official lie. Things haven't changed very much in the four hundred years since Henry Wotton described an ambassador as "an honest man sent to lie abroad for the commonwealth." [1]

However much people may detest official lies, to cry out against such deception is not really very helpful, nor even very Christian. There is, of course, a biblical precedent for denouncing deceit in high governmental office, but it is mostly in the Old Testament when the kingdom of Israel was a kind of theocracy. The king himself was drawn from the community of faith and subject to its discipline. In the New Testament Jesus and the apostles lived under corrupt Roman rule but had very little to say about the dishonesty of political leaders like Herod, Pilate, and Caesar. On the other hand, Jesus had a lot to say about the deceit of religious leaders (Matthew 23).

What may appear to be a double standard is actually the only sensible approach. All lying, governmental and individual, is wrong. But to attack the lies of people in high office diverts attention from our own temptations to deceive. The attack is unlikely to change anything in political life but it gets us off the hook. If you look closely, you are apt to find in yourself the same seeds of deceit you object to in others.

Tell the Whole Truth

The best liar is one who is able to make the smallest amount of lying go the furthest. Real experts can lie without saying anything untrue. For example, all of the statements of demons quoted in the Bible are true (e.g. Mark 1:23-24; 3:11; 5:6-7), but being masters of deceit, the demons use the truth to their own deceptive ends. The rest of us amateur liars bungle along.

After a fishing trip ended in total failure, the fisherman stopped at a fish market. "Just stand over there and throw me five of the biggest trout you've got," he said.

"Throw 'em?" asked the puzzled dealer. "Whatever for?"

"So I can tell my wife I caught them. I may be a poor fisher, but I'm no liar!"

That's what *he* thinks. He told the truth but not the whole truth. He is like the farmer who, being stricken by a guilty conscience, went to his neighbor and confessed, "I'm sorry I stole a rope from you last year."

"A rope? Think nothing of it, neighbor. Let's forget it and be friends."

But the farmer had no peace about it because he had neglected to tell the neighbor that there was a cow attached to the end of the rope when he stole it. Tell the truth, but be sure it is the whole truth.

A complete lie is easily killed, but a half-truth has nine lives. It is far more deceptive because it is more believable. Benjamin Disraeli said, "There are three kinds of lies: lies, damned lies and statistics."[2] It is statistical facts, carefully chosen and artfully arranged to deceive, that constitute the worst form of dishonesty.

Tell the Whole Truth in Love

Paul brings two important principles together in his letter to the Ephesians. "By speaking the truth in a spirit of love, we must grow up in every way to Christ . . ." (Ephesians 4:15). Whenever there is a conflict between truth and love, love should win.

One minister's family was given a mince pie for Christmas by a lady who was good-hearted but a poor cook. The pie was so dry and over-spiced that it had to be thrown out. Faced with the difficult task of being both truthful and kind, the minister said, "We appreciate your gift. And let me assure you that a mince pie like yours never lasts long at our house."

This was, of course, a clever piece of lying, but presumably the motive behind it makes it a little more acceptable. Most white lies, however, are told not for love but to avoid social embarrassment. Rahab provides us the best model of a white lie. She bore false witness against her neighbors in Jericho when they demanded the whereabouts of the Israelite spies (Joshua 2:1-7). Her behavior, though, was commendable because it kept the higher law of love. Whenever love and truth are in conflict, it is better to be on the side of love.

The Christian goes beyond the minimal requirements of honesty to speak the truth in love. Without truth, love becomes cheap "sloppy agape." It disintegrates into mere sentimental feeling. Without love, truth becomes brittle, cold facts that freeze the soul.

Scripture References for Further Study

What Saints Do in Respect to Lying:

Hate lies   *Psalm 119:163; Proverbs 13:5*
Avoid lies   *Isaiah 63:8; Zephaniah 3:13*
Reject lying   *Psalm 40:4, KJV*
Pray to be preserved from lying   *Psalm 119:29, KJV; Proverbs 30:8*

What Sinners Do in Respect to Lying:

Are addicted to lies   *Psalm 58:3*
Love lies   *Psalm 52:3*
Delight in lies   *Psalm 62:4*
Seek after false things   *Psalm 4:2*
Prepare their tongues for lying   *Jeremiah 9:3, 5*
Give heed to lies   *Proverbs 17:4*

What Satan Does in Respect to Lying:

Is the father of liars   *John 8:44*
Excites people to lie   *1 Kings 22:22; Acts 5:3*

Lying Leads to:

Hatred   *Proverbs 26:28*
Love of impure conversation   *Proverbs 17:4*
Gross crimes   *Hosea 4:1-2*

Consequences of Lying:

Lying is an abomination to God   *Proverbs 6:16-19; 12:22*
Lying is a hindrance to prayer   *Isaiah 59:2-3*
Exclusion from heaven   *Revelation 21:8, 27; 22:15*

Exclusion from fellowship   *Psalm 101:3-7*
Punishment by court   *Deuteronomy 19:15-21; Proverbs 19:5*
Punishment by God   *Psalm 120:3-4*
A liar is destroyed by God   *Psalm 5:6*

This Commandment Is Broken by:

False prophets   *Jeremiah 23:14; 50:36; Ezekiel 22:28*
False witnesses   *Proverbs 14:5, 25*
Antinomians   *1 John 1:6; 2:4*
Hypocrites   *Isaiah 57:4, KJV; Hosea 11:12*
Gossips   *Proverbs 11:13; 26:17-28*

Examples of Testimony in Court:

Honest testimony under duress   *Leviticus 19:16; 1 Samuel 22:6-19*
False testimony through bribery   *1 Kings 21:8-14; Matthew 26:59-61;
   Acts 6:11-13*

10

Sin That's Hard
to Live With

The Decalogue concludes with a commandment that few people take very seriously. Have you ever heard of anyone being punished for breaking the Tenth Commandment? People are hanged for breaking the Sixth and sued for breaking the Ninth, but nobody has ever paid a fine or gone to jail for coveting. No human law attempts to govern human attitudes, but God's law does. No detective could discover the Tenth Commandment's violation, but God can.

Not even the church takes the sin of greed very seriously. There are periodic attempts to boycott television programs that pander to depraved appetites for sex and violence, but who ever heard of a boycott of programs that pander to depraved appetites for wealth and opulence? Churches pass resolutions against the sin of intoxication by the spirit of alcohol, but where are the resolutions against the sin of intoxication by the spirit of greed? Some churches refuse to allow a person whose love for another made him or her divorce his or her spouse to serve as a church officer, but where is the church that rejects someone on the ground that that person's love of money has made him or her too ambitious? The rich young ruler is no longer offended by severe demands of Christlike living (Luke 18:18-23) but welcomed and made treasurer of the church.

The commandment says, "Thou shalt not covet," and it is likely that God intends this for our age even more than for the time in which it was originally given. Greed is certainly a greater problem for us today than for Moses and his rag-tag followers in 1400 B.C. One ancient Hebrew could hardly possess things any other Hebrew did not already have. One might have ten goats and another twenty, but goats are goats and are no big deal around which to build a strong case of covetousness. With few exceptions the entire Hebrew community shared the same standard of living and enjoyed equal opportunities.

Ah, but today we are blessed with a great abundance of goods with which to feed our greed. We have the technology to create an infinite variety of things that people want, and we have an advertising industry to make people want them. Add these two together, and we have a foundation for covetousness, the bedrock of our whole economy.

Greed Makes It Hard to Live with Ourselves

Our modern way of life has been so infected with greed that people find it hard to live with themselves. Humankind is the only species of the animal kingdom whose desires increase when they are fed. Fido, the family dog, wants no more now than did his ancestor who curled up beside the caveman's fire. The ox aspires to no more than did its fore-bears that pulled the first covered wagons across the western prairies. But the human species is discontent with the basics that once satisfied humans in an earlier age.

Wouldn't it be interesting to hear today's teenagers tell *their* children what they had to do without? Yesterday's luxuries become today's conveniences and tomorrow's necessities. It is trite but true: the more people have, the more people want. Lyndon B. Johnson spoke for all of the dissatisfied when he said, "All I want is all there is." Human hunger for worldly goods is insatiable.

"Satisfaction guaranteed" is a vain promise to those who set their hearts on possessions, power, or status. Covetous people play the game of life like Pac-Man: they gobble up all they can, but inevitably they are beaten and eaten. They can't win for losing. If they can't get what they want, they are frustrated; but if they do get what they want, they are quickly bored. The most bored people in the world are not the underprivileged but the overprivileged. They have everything to live with but not much to live for.

The Bible presents us with an intriguing set of paradoxes concerning material goods. They are good things (Luke 16:25), but we must not long for them (Colossians 3:5-7). They are to be enjoyed, but we must not make that enjoyment our goal. They are things we need (James 2:16), but we must not devote our lives to getting them (Matthew 6:31-32). The Savior gave loaves and fish to the multitudes (Matthew 14:15-21) but proclaimed that people do not live by bread alone (Matthew

4:4). He taught the disciples to pray, "Give us today the food we need" (Matthew 6:11) but warned, ". . . Do not be worried about the food and drink you need in order to stay alive, or about clothes for your body" (Matthew 6:25).

These paradoxes become a little easier to understand if we distinguish carefully between means and ends. Jesus said, "Seek ye first the kingdom of God . . . and all these things shall be added unto you" (Matthew 6:33, KJV). His kingdom is our end goal; everything else is a means of achieving it. Worldly goods are valued for the way they contribute to the kingdom of God. If they do not contribute, then they are worthless or worse. Material goods can be a currency of love, a means by which people share love with one another and in which people discover the love of God. We are to desire no more of them than we can get justly, use wisely, distribute cheerfully, and leave contentedly.

Greed Makes It Hard To Live with Others

The greedy person doesn't really enjoy having anything. What gives him or her pleasure is having *more* than someone else. Poverty is a state of mind induced by a neighbor's new car, stereo, pool, and so on.

There is profound wisdom in Aesop's parable of the greedy man. Zeus promised to grant him any wish *provided* that his neighbor got twice as much. He could wish for a mansion, but his neighbor would get a castle. He could wish for twenty cows, but his neighbor would get forty. The story ends with the man wishing to lose one eye!

Roland Diller, one of Abraham Lincoln's neighbors in Springfield, wrote about an incident that happened in his early life. Called to his door by the cries of children in the street, he saw Lincoln striding by with two of his boys, both of whom were wailing aloud. "Why, Mr. Lincoln, what's the matter with the boys?" he asked.

"Just what's the matter with the whole world," he answered. "I've got three walnuts, and each wants two."

That is, indeed, what is wrong with the whole world. Greed makes it hard to live with others because a person filled with greed sees other persons as competitors for prominence instead of partners in progress. Thus, greed destroys fellowship. Greed creates a hell on earth—no satisfaction, no security, no peace, only the constant discontent of selfish desire.

However bad a generous person may be, some will like him or her (e.g. Robin Hood and Jesse James). But however good a greedy person may be, all will detest him or her. Generosity covers a multitude of vices, but greed cancels a multitude of virtues. A miser may be valued as an ancestor but not as a neighbor.

Greed Makes It Hard to Live with God

Not only does greed make it hard to live with ourselves and others, but greed also makes it hard to live with God. Greed leads to the breaking of the first four commandments. Greed causes people to invent substitute gods, giving them attractive images (Ephesians 5:5). Unsatisfied desire curses people and circumstances and destroys the Sabbath rest. Thus, the greedy person smashes the first commandment of the law and breaks off his or her relationship with God.

Greed makes it hard to live with God because greed is completely contrary to God's nature. God is infinitely generous. "He gives rain to those who do good and to those who do evil" (Matthew 5:45). However, there can be no fellowship between two people who are guided by diametrically opposite principles. There can be no companionship between God whose heart is afire with love and a person whose heart is frozen with greed.

Greed makes it hard to live with God. When a greedy person prays, it is not to seek God's will but to enlist his help in supplying selfish desires. That person seeks God not for himself, but so that he or she can hire God as a night watchman for mammon.

Where, then, can one find the contentment that overcomes covetousness? Certainly not in a simple reassurance that one doesn't need what one wants. The fortress of desire is far too strong for that. Only a greater love can displace the deadly desire of covetousness. Paul advises the Corinthians to "Covet earnestly the best gifts" (1 Corinthians 12:31, KJV). The best gifts are not a neighbor's car, house, or wife but wisdom, kindness, courtesy, and honesty. Paul says, ". . . Set your hearts on the things that are in heaven. . . . Keep your minds on things there, not on things here on earth . . . put to death, then, the earthly desires at work in you, such as sexual immorality, indecency, lust, evil passions, and greed" (Colossians 3:1-5). The only thing that can conquer the strong desire of greed is the stronger desire for better things. ". . . Fill your minds with those things that are good and that deserve praise: things that are true, noble, right, pure, lovely, and honorable" (Philippians 4:8-9).

Scripture References for Further Study

Greed Comes from:

The heart *Mark 7:21-23; 2 Peter 2:14*
The attractiveness of the forbidden *Romans 7:8*

Greed Leads to:

Injustice *Micah 2:2*
Foolishness *1 Timothy 6:9*
Apostasy *Psalm 10:3; 1 Timothy 6:10*
Lying *2 Kings 5:20-27; 2 Peter 2:3*
Murder *Proverbs 1:18-19; Ezekiel 22:12*
Theft *Joshua 7:20-21; Micah 2:2*
Poverty *Proverbs 28:22*
Misery *1 Timothy 6:10*
Dissatisfaction *Ecclesiastes 5:10; Habakkuk 2:5*

Greed Is Described as:

Idolatry *Ephesians 5:5; Colossians 3:5*
Root of evil *Genesis 3:6; 1 Timothy 6:10*
Vanity *Psalm 39:6, KJV; Ecclesiastes 4:8, KJV*
Temporary *1 John 2:17*

Greed Is Characteristic of:

The wicked *Romans 1:29*
The slothful *Proverbs 21:25-26*
False teachers *2 Peter 2:3*
The last days *2 Timothy 3:1-2; 2 Peter 2:1-3*

What Saints Do with Respect to Greed:

Desire obedience more than riches *Psalm 119:36*
Be content with what they have *Hebrews 13:5-6*
Do not mention greed *Ephesians 5:3*
Put to death greedy desires *Colossians 3:5-7*
Beware of greed *Luke 12:13-15*
Avoid associating with greedy people *1 Corinthians 5:11*

Greed Is Punished by:

Destruction *Isaiah 5:8-10; Jeremiah 22:13-17; Micah 2:1-4*
Abandonment *Isaiah 57:17*

Exclusion from heaven   *1 Corinthians 6:10; Ephesians 5:5*

Greed Is Avoided by:

Purification of the heart   *Mark 7:20-23*
Contentment   *1 Timothy 6:6-10; Philippians 4:11-13*
Coveting only the best   *Psalm 37:3-4; Colossians 3:1-4; Philippians 4:8-9*

11

Love Your God

The Pharisees loved to argue. They were so fond of controversy that they wouldn't eat food that agreed with them. You know the type. If someone said the cup was half full, they would hotly contend that it was half empty. They loved to debate anything, but especially religious matters.

Their chief opponents in religious disputes were the Sadducees. Meetings between the two groups ended in shouting matches (see Acts 23:6-10). They hated each other and lost no opportunity for verbal combat.

Neither of these groups got along with Jesus. They wanted him to choose up sides, but he wouldn't play their game. He would answer their questions briefly and brilliantly and without being contentious.

One day when Jesus had stumped the Sadducees, the Pharisees turned on him, the new champ, to score a point or two. "When the Pharisees heard that Jesus had silenced the Sadducees, they came together, and one of them, a teacher of the Law, tried to trip him with a question. [Note that the challenger was no rookie debater, but the best they had.] 'Teacher,' he asked, 'which is the greatest commandment in the Law?'" (Matthew 22:34-36).

Now at least we must give the Pharisees credit for asking a serious question. Debating this issue was better than debating whether Adam had a navel or many other questions that have preoccupied the minds of theological gladiators. The answer to their question would make a real difference in the way one behaved. For example, suppose that a man named Cornelius is arrested and charged with treason by the Roman authorities. His son, Romulus, knows that his father is, in fact, part of a conspiracy against the hated Caesar. He is asked to testify at his father's trial. The question he faces is should he break the Fifth Commandment and dishonor his father or should he break the Ninth Commandment and bear false witness? Which is the greater commandment?

When a little boy was asked why he stole an apple, he explained, "I couldn't stop coveting the apple; so I decided to go on and steal it." But is stealing worse than coveting? Is the Sixth Commandment more important than the Tenth? How do you know? What is the greatest commandment in the Law?

In answer to the Pharisee's question Jesus quoted the *Shema,* the basic creed of Judaism, the John-three-sixteen of the Jews, the first verse every Jewish child learns. It is the Scripture quoted to open every Jewish worship service even to this present time: "Hear, O Israel: The Lord our God, the Lord is one; and you shall love the Lord your God with all your heart, with all your soul, and with all your mind, and with all your strength" (Mark 12:29-30, RSV).

Although the commandment that Jesus quoted was not one of the Ten, it clearly sums up and deepens the first four commandments. Our love for God makes it unthinkable for us to give our hearts to attractive images of substitute gods and to dishonor God's name and day of worship. To love God is the greatest and most important commandment.

Love Your God with All of Your Heart

How long has it been since you were deeply touched by the Lord your God? To love God with all of your heart necessarily involves your emotions. The emotionally disturbed are not only those who have too much emotion but also those who show too little emotion and who fear their feelings. They are like the sunburn victim who replied to the question "How are you feeling?" with, "Far too much!"

In worship we must tread the narrow path between formalism and fanaticism, between too much and too little feeling. Emotion is like fire in the furnace. When it is contained and controlled, it provides warmth for the room. But if it escapes the furnace, it can burn down the house.

A person can't know God without involving his or her emotions. James asks, "Do you believe that there is only one God?" Assuming a positive answer, he scornfully says, "Good! The demons also believe—and tremble with fear" (James 2:19). A faith that doesn't tremble is even more phony than the belief of demons.

There can be no faith without feeling. "Now that we have been put right with God through faith, we have peace with God. . . . He has brought us by faith into this *experience* . . ." (Romans 5:1-2, author's italics). Christianity is not just a good idea, but it is a real experience with the living God. This experience, therefore, necessarily involves our emotions. We don't authenticate God when we have emotional feelings about him. Rather, we feel emotionally because God is revealed to us and relates to us. "This is the LORD's doing; it is marvelous in our eyes" (Psalm 118:23, KJV).

Love Your God with All Your Mind

Not only must you love God with all your heart, but also with all your mind. How long has it been since your mind was stretched in pondering the mysteries of the Lord your God? A lot of mistakes are due to people's feeling when they ought to think and thinking when they ought to feel.

It makes me a little nervous to hear a mechanic say, "I feel that your car's problem is a defective carburetor." I'm not paying him to feel, but to think as precisely and accurately as possible. Someone else may say, "I think Grand Ole Opry is better than grand opera," but thinking has nothing to do with his opinion. It's feeling that he's talking about.

When it comes to God, we must both feel deeply and think clearly. There is no spiritual value to muddled thinking about the Lord. The One who made our minds intends for us to use them to think as clearly as we can.

It is, of course, a challenge of colossal dimension.

> "'My thoughts,' says the LORD,
> 'are not like yours,
> and my ways are different
> from yours.
> As high as the heavens are
> above the earth,
> so high are my ways and
> thoughts above yours.'"
> Isaiah 55:8-9

Because the human mind cannot comprehend the Maker, however, is no excuse for not making the effort. Because a person can't drink a river dry is no reason why one can't satisfy one's immediate thirst.

To love God with all one's mind doesn't mean one has to be a know-it-all. Paul writes, "Although being a 'know-it-all' makes us feel important, what is really needed to build the church is love. If anyone thinks he knows all the answers, he is just showing his ignorance. But the person who truly loves God is the one who is open to God's knowledge'' (1 Corinthians 8:1-3, *Living Bible*).

If the fear of God is the beginning of knowledge, the love of God is its conclusion. John declares, ''Whoever does not love does not know God, for God is love'' (1 John 4:8). It's so clear; how could anyone miss it? Yet even some of the truly great theologians do. John Calvin wrote four hundred pages on the knowledge of God in which he quoted over eight hundred Scripture passages but never once referred to 1 John 4:8. What a pity! And what a shame that there are Christians today who may *study* God with their minds but who may neglect to *love* God with their minds.

Love Your God with All Your Soul

The third way you are to love God is with all your soul. The Greek word used for soul is *psyche*. It refers to the nonmaterial part of people that activates the physical. Without a soul the body won't *do* anything. To love God with all your soul is to love God in what you do. How long has it been since you did something courageous because you love the Lord your God? Love—either because-love or anyhow-love—puts on its overalls and goes to work.

Because-Love

Jesus said of the woman who washed his feet with her tears and dried them with her hair, ''. . . The great love she has shown proves that her many sins have been forgiven. But whoever has been forgiven little shows only a little love'' (Luke 7:47). The woman had a good reason to love the Lord, and so do we. In the words of an anonymous writer:

> You ask me why I love my Lord?
>   Well, friend, just let me say,
> Life wasn't worth the living
>   Till the Savior came my way.
> You say I miss so much of life;
>   Yes, friend, praise God I do!
> I miss the sin and sorrow
>   Which were all I ever knew.
> I miss the heavy burden
>   That I carried through the years.
> But, friend, I wouldn't have them back
>   For all that you could pay;
> Life wasn't worth the living
>   Till the Savior came my way.

Although Christ's promised rewards to us are real and reliable, remember that it is not the gifts we love but the Giver. An ancient legend tells of a woman walking down the road, holding a torch in one hand and a bucket of water in the other.

"What are those for?" someone asked.

"With this torch," she said, "I am going to burn up the mansions in heaven and with this water I will quench the fires of hell so that men will love God for the sake of God being God and not for want of the mansions or fear of the fire."

That was the attitude of the great missionary, Francis Xavier, who wrote over four hundred years ago:

> "My God, I love thee, not because I hope for heaven thereby,
> Nor yet because who love thee not are lost eternally;
> Not with the hope of gaining aught; not seeking a reward;
> But as thyself hast loved me, O ever-loving Lord,
> E'en so I love thee, and will love, and in thy praise will sing,
> Solely because thou art my God, and my eternal King."

Because-love is based on motives that may be either selfish or selfless. There is another kind of love, however, that does not look for causes. It is a pure gift.

Anyhow-Love

The prophet Habakkuk faced the loss of all the customary reasons to love God and concluded his book of prophecy saying,

> Even though the fig trees have
> no fruit
> and no grapes grow on the
> vines,
> even though the olive crop
> fails
> and the fields produce no
> grain,
> even though the sheep all die
> and the cattle stalls are
> empty,
> I will still be joyful and glad,
> because the LORD God is my
> savior.
>
> Habakkuk 3:17

Love is not just something one feels and thinks; it is something one does. One of the dictionary definitions of "love" is "no points scored" as in tennis, "love-forty." Does your life reveal this to be the definition of your love for God? Does your record say, "Lord, you haven't scored any points"? Are you even in the game?

> Teach me to love Thee as Thine angels love,
> One holy passion filling all my frame;
> The baptism of the heaven-descended Dove,
> My heart an altar, and thy love the flame.[1]

Scripture References for Further Study

Love for God Is Produced by:

An obedient heart given to us   *Deuteronomy 30:6*
The Holy Spirit within us   *Romans 5:5; Galatians 5:22; 2 Thessalonians 3:5, KJV*
God's love for us   *1 John 4:19*

Our Love for God Should Produce:

Joy   *Psalm 5:11, KJV*
Love   *1 John 4:19*
Obedience   *John 14:15; 1 John 2:5; 5:2-5*
Courage   *1 John 4:17-18*

In Regard to Loving God, Saints Should:

Persevere in love   *Jude, v. 21*
Grow in understanding of God's love   *2 Thessalonians 3:5*

Those Who Love God:

Are known by God   *1 Corinthians 8:3*
Are saved by God   *Psalm 91:14*
Are protected by God   *Psalm 5:11; 145:20*
Are loved by God   *Exodus 20:6; Deuteronomy 7:9*
Do not love the world   *1 John 2:15*
Have all things working for their good   *Romans 8:28*
Are promised
  food to eat   *Deuteronomy 11:13-15*
  a place to live   *Psalm 69:35-36*
  a crown of life   *James 1:12, KJV*

Types of People Who Are Unable to Love God:

Those who do not love others   *1 John 4:20*
Those who are hypocrites   *Luke 11:42; John 5:42*

Those who are uncharitable   *1 John 3:17*

Our Love of God Is:

Commanded   *Deuteronomy 10:12-13; 11:1; Joshua 22:5; Matthew 22:37-38*
Exemplified by Christ   *John 14:31*
Tested by God   *Deuteronomy 13:2-3*

Our Love for God Is More Important than:

Any act of religious sacrifice   *Mark 12:33*
Our love for any object   *Deuteronomy 6:5; Matthew 22:37-38*

12

Love Your Neighbor

Peppermint Patty said to Charlie Brown, "I don't understand. I thought the new law said that dogs have to be kept tied."

Charlie Brown replied, "There are some things that are stronger than rope, you know. I have Snoopy tied up with a feeling of obligation."

Coming to the end of this book, you also may be tied up with feelings of obligation. The apostle Paul simplifies things by declaring,

> . . . The only obligation you have is to love one another. Whoever does this has obeyed the Law. The commandments, "Do not commit adultery; do not commit murder; do not steal; do not desire what belongs to someone else"—all these, and any others besides, are summed up in the one command, "Love your neighbor as you love yourself" (Romans 13:8-9).

Jesus made it clear that the command to love God is more important than the command to love a neighbor (Matthew 22:37-40). But the apostle John claims that a person can't love one without loving the other. "If someone says he loves God, but hates his brother, he is a liar. For he cannot love God, whom he has not seen, if he does not love his brother, whom he has seen. The command that Christ has given us is this: whoever loves God must love his brother also" (1 John 4:20).

If John means that loving a visible neighbor is much easier than loving the invisible God, I think he has the situation backwards from the actual experience of most people. It may be easy to love God precisely because we have not seen him. And we'd probably be able to love our "pesky" brothers and neighbors, too, if we didn't see so much of them. It may be that seeing is believing, but seeing is not necessarily loving. Sometimes the neighbor's mannerisms keep building up irritations until we detest the neighbor.

The Bible makes it clear, though: I must love my neighbor specifically, not just humanity in general. It would be easy for me to love a pygmy. I don't know any pygmies. I have an abstract picture of them that passes for reality in my mind.

But my love for them is no more honest than the man who found his children's tracks in freshly poured cement. As he raged at them, his wife asked, "Don't you love the children?"

"Of course, I love the children in the abstract," he said, "but not in the concrete!"

Yet it is in the concrete that we must love one another in spite of the difficulty of doing that. As one exasperated Christian put it,

> To live in love with the saints above—
> Oh, that would be glory
> But to live below with the saints we know—
> Oh, that's a different story![1]

One of America's favorite philosophers, Charlie Brown, said, "I'm going to be a doctor when I grow up."

Lucy argued, "But you can't. To be a doctor, you have to love humanity."

"I do love humanity," Charlie said, "It's people I can't stand."

In C. S. Lewis's *Screwtape Letters,* Screwtape, a senior executive demon, advises Wormwood, a junior demon,

But do what you will, there is going to be some benevolence, as well as some malice, in your patient's soul. The great thing is to direct the malice to his immediate neighbours whom he meets every day and to thrust his benevolence out to the remote circumference, to people he does not know. The malice thus becomes wholly real and the benevolence largely imaginary.[2]

Perhaps the real point of 1 John 4:20 is not that one of the two commandments is more difficult than the other but that one is the truer test of love. Our love of the invisible God is largely imaginary unless it is tested and demonstrated by our love of visible neighbors. It is impossible to check the water level in a large boiler by looking into it. But attached to the boiler is a tiny glass tube that serves as a gauge of the water level in the boiler. The water level in the tube indicates the water level in the boiler. The water in the boiler is our love for God; the water level in the tube is our love of neighbor, the gauge of our love for God.

Within the acorn of love lies the giant oak of humanitarian service. To attempt to love a neighbor without first responding to God's love is like trying to grow an oak by planting an oak leaf. But beginning from an acorn of love, a healthy tree will not fail to produce strong branches of service to others.

Love Your Neighbor Because He or She Needs It

Your neighbor needs your love for his or her survival. The world has become one neighborhood before people have learned to live like neighbors. Modern communication and transportation have shrunk the world, but the human family is falling apart. People can talk by radio, telephone, and television to almost anyone on earth; but the more people talk, the less people seem to understand. Humankind has created a modern Babel. People can go anywhere on earth in a few hours, but much of the world has the unwelcome mat out.

Historian Arnold Toynbee said, "The difference is not an ethical one, but a practical one. In the pre-atomic age, our failure to love our enemies was morally wrong. . . . But in the atomic age the practical consequences are going to be suicidal." [3]

People need love not only for survival but also for their personal growth and change. Your experience may be like mine. I have discovered that the most influential people in my life have not been those who didn't like me the way I was and tried to change me into something more agreeable to them. Rather, the most influential people in my life have been those who loved me as I was and provided a winsome model for me that changed my life. The gospel declares that Christ loves us unconditionally. But when we respond to his love, we can never be the same. His love changes us into more Christlike people.

The power of love is found in its penetration. It is undeflected by the superficial facts about people. Instead it penetrates to their possibilities. The facts can be unlovely, but the possibilities are always as bright as the promises of God.

Love your neighbor because he or she needs your love for personal change and growth. Pierre Teilhard de Chardin said, "Some day, after we have mastered the winds, the waves, the tides and gravity, we will harness for God the energies of love and then for the second time in the history of the world man will have discoverd fire." [4]

Love Your Neighbor Because You Need to Do So

People were created with the capacity and the need for love. Without love a person is as incomplete as a car without a crankshaft. It is possible to be as straight as a drinking straw ethically and as empty as a drinking straw spiritually. Paul's point in the great love chapter, 1 Corinthians 13, is that nothing a person does has any value unless it is done with love—not inspired preaching, not mountain-moving faith, not sacrificial giving—nothing is worth anything unless it is motivated by love.

Mother Teresa of Calcutta, Nobel Prize winning humanitarian, said, "Each one has a mission to fulfill, a mission of love. At the hour of death when we come face to face with God, we are going to be judged on love; not how much we have done, but how much love we have put into our actions."

The circumference of one's soul is measured by the radius of one's love. Nature says, "Love yourself"; romance says, "Love your sweetheart"; marriage says, "Love your family"; patriotism says, "Love your country"; Christ says, "Love everybody. Any friend of God's is a friend of mine." And God loves the world.

Love is the Christian's badge, his or her mark of identity. "If you have love for one another," Jesus said, "then everyone will know that you are my disciples" (John 13:35). We love our neighbor not because of who he or she is but because of who we are: objects and subjects of God's love. "We love because God first loved us" (1 John 4:19).

Your love for your neighbor must be of the same quality as your love for yourself and Christ's love for you and God's love for Christ. Jesus said, "I love you just as the Father loves me; remain in my love . . . love one another, just as I love you" (John 15:9-12).

What God has done for you becomes what you must do for God through your neighbor. The Scripture calls on you to give your life for others as Christ has given his life for you (1 John 3:16), to forgive them as you have been forgiven (Ephesians 4:32), and to serve them as you have been served (John 13:14-15).

Scripture References for Further Study

In Regard to Love Saints Should:

Put on love   *Colossians 3:14*
Strive for love   *1 Corinthians 14:1*
Let their love grow   *Philippians 1:9; 1 Thessalonians 3:12*
Continue to love   *Hebrews 13:1*
Help one another to show love   *Hebrews 10:24*
Be sincere in love   *Romans 12:9; 2 Corinthians 6:6; 8:8; 1 John 3:18*
Be unselfish in love   *1 Corinthians 10:24; 13:5; Philippians 2:4*

Be fervent in love   *1 Peter 1:22; 4:8*

Love Is Shown Toward:

Saints   *1 Peter 2:17; 1 John 5:1-2*
Pastors   *1 Thessalonians 5:13*
Families   *Ephesians 5:21–6:4; Titus 2:4*
Strangers   *Leviticus 19:34; Deuteronomy 10:19*
Enemies   *Exodus 23:4-5; 2 Kings 6:22; Matthew 5:44; Romans 12:14, 20; 1 Peter 3:9*
Everyone   *Galatians 6:10*

Love Is Shown in:

Meeting needs of others   *Matthew 25:35; Hebrews 6:10*
Sympathizing with others   *Romans 12:15; 1 Corinthians 12:26*
Supporting the weak   *Galatians 6:2; 1 Thessalonians 5:14*
Forgiving offenders   *Proverbs 10:12; Ephesians 4:32; Colossians 3:13; 1 Peter 4:8*
Being patient and tolerant   *Ephesians 4:2*
Being kind   *Romans 12:10; 2 Peter 1:7*
All activities   *1 Corinthians 16:14*

Love Is Evidence of:

Enlightenment   *1 John 2:10*
Discipleship   *John 13:35; Romans 8:9*
Life   *1 John 3:14*

Love Is Motivated by:

Love of God   *1 John 4:11*
Fruit of the Spirit   *Galatians 5:22*
Love of Christ   *2 Corinthians 5:14*
Command of Christ   *John 13:34; 15:12; 1 John 3:23*
Example of Christ   *Ephesians 5:2*

Love Is Superior to:

Supernatural gifts   *1 Corinthians 13:1, 2*
Personal sacrifice   *1 Corinthians 13:3*
Faith and hope   *1 Corinthians 13:13*

What Love Does:

Casts out fear   *1 John 4:18*
Fulfills the Law   *Romans 13:8-10; Galatians 5:14; James 2:8*
Binds all things together   *Colossians 2:2; 3:14*
Works Hard   *1 Thessalonians 1:3; Galatians 5:6; Hebrews 6:10*

13

Love Yourself

Sometimes there is more truth in the funny papers than on the front page of the paper. Cartoons often express a profound truth of the human condition—an integrated understanding of the issues behind the front page facts. For example, in one cartoon a doctor with a worried expression on his face says to a patient, "This is a very serious case. I believe you are allergic to yourself!" The truth is, we are all in that poor guy's condition—allergic to ourselves!

"Love yourself" is *not* an explicit command. It is an implicit assumption in Jesus' commandment, "Love your neighbor as you love yourself" (Matthew 22:39). Self-love is not a virtue that Christ commended but a fact that he recognized and told us to use as a standard. The best commentary on the "second great commandment" is the so-called golden rule: "Do for others what you want them to do for you" (Matthew 7:12).

Although self-love may have been a safe assumption in Jesus' day, it is no longer. Lewis B. Smedes, professor of theology and ethics at Fuller Theological Seminary says,

> Anyone who can see the needs of people today must recognize that the malaise of our time is an epidemic of self-doubt and self-depreciation. Those whose job it is to heal people's spiritual problems know that the overwhelming majority of people who seek help are people who are sick from abhorring themselves. A prevailing sense of being without worth is the depressive sickness of our age.[1]

Alcoholism, drug addiction, stomach ulcers, suicide, and mental illness often have one common denominator: self-hate.

Self-Hating

Self-hate is one of the roots of sinful pride. Those who hate themselves erect a wall of arrogance to shield themselves from the adverse opinions of others. Conceit is compensation for the lack of self-value. When those who believe in reincarnation talk about their previous lives, have you noticed how often they claim to have been a king, a queen, or a crusader? Nobody says that he or she swept up after the chariot races!

But those who truly love themselves don't have to display their virtues in sinful pride. They don't need to treasure their goodness like a private trophy of something that isn't real. They are serenely quiet about it all.

It is sometimes said of a vain proud person, "I wish I could buy him for what he is worth and sell him for what he thinks he is worth." But I'll tell you an even better deal: buy that person for what he or she thinks he or she is worth and sell that person for what he or she pretends to be worth.

If sinful pride is the person's problem, criticizing the person is not the answer. Criticism, in fact, creates pride more often than it creates humility. The more persons are criticized, the greater are their needs to pretend to virtue. They vainly try to push themselves ahead by patting themselves on the back. If persons are pressed too far by criticism, they will finally lose their self-respect.

Genuine compliments, on the other hand, usually create humility. Parents, praise your children's good marks, good looks, and good behavior. They'll work much harder to live up to your expectations and have less pride doing it. Husbands, compliment your wives. Wives, show your appreciation for your husbands. Build people up. Don't tear people down. Praise doesn't make people proud, but humble.

Self-Seeking

Although self-hate is the problem, self-seeking is not the answer. Seeking one's own advantage is a universal, chronic human disorder. Jesus rebuked the people of his day who drew attention to themselves by their ostentatious clothing, fancy titles, and prominent seats in the synagogue. He warned them and us, "Whoever makes himself great will be humbled, and whoever humbles himself will be made great" (Matthew 23:12).

One of the signs of decadence in the "last days" will be that "people will be selfish, greedy, boastful, and conceited" (2 Timothy 3:2). Paul declares that all such people will suffer God's anger (Ephesians 2:3).

To seek one's personal advantage turns oneself into an idol to which all other values are sacrificed. Paul Vitz in his book, *Psychology as Religion: The Cult of Self-Worship,* writes, "To worship one's self (in self-realization) . . . is, in Christian terms, simple idolatry operating from the usual motive of unconscious egotism."[2]

The idolatry of "self" has become the latest psychological fad. Social scientist Daniel Yankelovich writes, ". . . In place of the old self-denial ethic we find people who refuse to deny *anything* to themselves—not out of bottomless appetite, but on the strange moral principle that 'I have a duty to myself.'"[3]

This miserable world is becoming populated with little Jack Horners who sit in their private corners eating their Christmas pie. They stick in their thumb and pull out a plum and say, "What a good boy am I!"

Of course, they don't really believe it. Their problem is self-hate. All of their attempts at self-righteousness are futile (Luke 16:15). The answer to self-hate is not self-seeking, but self-love.

Self-Loving

There is in English, unfortunately, no positive adjective from the word "self." There is only "selfish" which is negative in meaning. From the word "child" there are two adjectives, "childish" and "childlike." The English language recognizes a good side and a bad side to acting like a child. I wish the same were true of "self," for it, too, has a good side and a bad side. We need the word "selfish" to describe the vices of the self-seeking person, but we ought to have a word such as "self-like" or "self-love" to describe the one who accepts and appreciates his or her true self as a unique gift of God.

Self-Love Enables Neighbor-Love

Loving one's neighbor is too risky for those who hate themselves. Love begins with self-disclosure, entrusting to the care of another person one's secret self. But those who believe themselves to be fundamentally unlikable are afraid to unmask their souls. When John Powell, who wrote the best-seller *Why Am I Afraid to Tell You Who I Am?* was asked that question by an acquaintance, he answered, "If I tell you who I am, you may not like who I am, and it's all I have."

One person can love another person only to the extent that one loves oneself. Samuel Johnson put his finger on this problem when he said, "I hate mankind; for I think myself one of the best of them and I know how bad I am."

God's Love Enables Self-Love

John wrote, "We love [self, neighbor, and God] because he first loved us" (1 John 4:19). When a person discovers that God loves unconditionally, by grace alone, that person is set free to love himself or herself and others on the same basis.

By beginning with God's love one is delivered from the ancient Pelagian heresy of trying to pull oneself up by one's own bootstraps. God has designed the human psyche in such a way that pulling on one's bootstraps doesn't get a person off the ground but doubles one up into a ball. What a person needs, of course, is a point of leverage. Archimedes claimed that given a strong enough fulcrum, he could move the world. A person's self-esteem can be moved only if there is a fulcrum, a reference point outside one's self. God's love is that reference point.

A person's value cannot be acquired by anything he or she does but rather by something God does. It cannot be earned; it is a free gift. It must be obtained because it cannot be attained.

A prize-winning weight lifter once boasted of his great strength. A gardener said, "I bet you twenty-five dollars that I can wheel a load in this wheelbarrow across the street and that you can't wheel it back."

"You're on," said the strong man. "What's your load?"

"Get in," said the gardener.

You can't carry yourself. Your self-esteem must be accepted as a divine gift. God doesn't love you because you are important. You are important because God loves you.

Abraham Lincoln said, "It is difficult to make a man miserable while he feels he is worthy of himself and claims kindred to the great God who made him."[4] That's the answer to all of our miserable self-hate and self-seeking. God freely gives worth to each creature. The One who made the stars, the mountains, and the seas reached out of eternity and said, "I want you." You are handpicked by the Creator of the universe. You are a precious jewel awaiting your mounting from God (Malachi 3:17, KJV).

The goal of creation is not merely a good world but good people. God is in the process of making men and women who are his sons and daughters and will share his love and glory forever. All the rest is scenery.

John declares,

See how much the Father has loved us! His love is so great that we are called God's children—and so in fact, we are. . . . My dear friends, we are now God's children, but it is not yet clear what we shall become. But we know that when Christ appears, we shall be like him, because we shall see him as he really is. Everyone who has this hope in Christ keeps himself pure, just as Christ is pure (1 John 3:1-3).

We are Christians under construction. The walls are unpainted and ugly scaffolding is still in place, but, praise God, he's not finished with us yet!

Scripture References for Further Study

Self-Examination Is:

Asked for   *Psalm 26:2; 139:23-24*
Commanded   *1 Corinthians 11:28; 2 Corinthians 13:5; Galatians 6:4-5*
Rewarded   *Lamentations 3:19-24; 1 Corinthians 11:31-32*
Performed honestly   *Romans 12:3*
Accompanied by
   resolution   *Psalm 119:59*
   self-confidence   *1 John 3:20-21*

Self-Denial Is:

Necessary
   in following Christ   *Luke 14:27-33*
   in winning the victory   *1 Corinthians 9:25-27*
Exemplified by
   Abraham   *Genesis 13:8-9; Hebrews 11:8-9*
   Moses   *Hebrews 11:24-25*
   Esther   *Esther 4:16*
   Rechabites   *Jeremiah 35:6-7*
   Daniel   *Daniel 1:8-16*
   Apostles   *Matthew 19:27*
   Barnabas   *Acts 4:36-37*
   Christ   *Matthew 4:3-10; 8:20; John 6:38; Romans 15:3; 2 Corinthians 8:9; Philippians 2:6-11*
Exercised in
   resisting natural lusts   *Romans 6:12-13; Titus 2:12; 1 Peter 2:11; 4:2*
   getting rid of the old self   *Ephesians 4:22; Colossians 3:9-10*
   not pleasing ourselves   *Romans 15:1-3*
   not seeking our own advantage   *1 Corinthians 10:24, 33; 13:4-5; Philippians 2:4*

crucifixion   *Romans 6:6; Galatians 5:24; 6:14*
Rewarded by
  finding self   *Matthew 16:24-25*
  sharing the divine nature   *2 Peter 1:3-4*
  truly living   *Romans 8:12-13*

Self-Seeking Is:

Forbidden   *1 Corinthians 10:24; Philippians 2:4*
Futile   *Luke 16:15*
Inconsistent with
  love   *1 Corinthians 13:4-5*
  communion   *1 Corinthians 12:12-27*
  redemption   *2 Corinthians 5:14-15*
Characteristic of
  the spiritually dead   *Ephesians 2:1-3*
  the last days   *2 Timothy 3:1-2*
Exemplified in
  Cain   *Genesis 4:9*
  Nabal   *1 Samuel 25:3-11*
  Haman   *Esther 6:6*
  James and John   *Mark 10:37*
  Pharisees   *Matthew 23:1-12*

We Have Self-Value Because We Are:

Made in God's image   *Genesis 1:27*
God's precious jewel   *Malachi 3:17, KJV*
Inferior only to God   *Psalm 8:5*
God's special creation   *Psalm 139:13-18*
God's children   *1 John 3:1-2*
Made right with God   *Romans 5:1-2*

Notes

Introduction

[1] Horatius Bonar, *God's Way of Holiness* (New York: Robert Carter & Brothers, 1870), p. 126.

Chapter 1

[1] Joy Davidman, *Smoke on the Mountain* (Philadelphia: The Westminster Press, 1953), p. 23.
[2] *The Confessions of St. Augustine* (New York: Liveright Publishing Corp., n.d.), p. 1.
[3] C. S. Lewis, *The Problem of Pain* (New York: Macmillan, Inc., 1940), p. 68.

Chapter 2

[1] Joy Davidman, *Smoke on the Mountain* (Philadelphia: The Westminster Press, 1953), p. 34.
[2] C. S. Lewis, "Footnote to All Prayers," *Poems* (London: Geoffey Bles, 1964), p. 129.
[3] J. G. Frazier, *Psyche's Task*, 2nd. ed. (New York: Macmillan, Inc., 1913), p. 5.

Chapter 3

[1] C. S. Lewis, *Pilgrim's Regress* (Grand Rapids: Wm. B. Eerdmans Publishing Co., 1945), p. 184. Used by permission.

Chapter 4

[1] Alan Richardson, *The Biblical Doctrine of Work* (London: SCM Press Ltd., 1952), p. 22.
[2] John Sullivan Dwight, *Leaves of Gold*, ed. Clyde F. Lytle (n.p.: Coslett Publishing Co., 1948). Used by permission of Brownlow Publishing Co.
[3] Jill Brisco at Festival of Evangelism in Kansas City, July 9, 1981.

Chapter 6

[1] Secretary of Health, Education, and Welfare, *Alcohol and Health* (June, 1978), p. v.
[2] Vernard Eller, *The Mad Morality* (Nashville: Abingdon Press, 1970), p. 49.

Chapter 7

[1] Bradley S. Breenberg, Robert Abelman, Kimberly Neuendorf, "Sex on the Soap Operas: Afternoon Delight," *Journal of Communication* (Summer 1981) vol. 31, no. 3.
[2] "Jews given sanction to hear women sing," *Topeka Capital-Journal*, December 21, 1975.

Chapter 8

[1] From the hymn, "There Is a Fountain" by William Cowper.

Chapter 9

[1] Henry Wotton, *Reliquiae Wottonianae*, as quoted in John Bartlett, *Familiar Quotations*, 8th ed. (Boston: Little, Brown, and Co., 1955), p. 144.
[2] Benjamin D'Israeli, as cited by *The Oxford Dictionary of Quotations*, 3rd. ed. (Oxford: Oxford University Press, 1979), p. 187.

Chapter 11

[1] From the hymn, "Spirit of God, Descend upon My Heart" by George Croly.

Chapter 12

[1] Quoted from a sermon given by Roy Paslay in Topeka, Kansas, 1973.
[2] C. S. Lewis, *Screwtape Letters* (Old Tappan, New Jersey: Fleming H. Revell Co., 1964), p. 43.
[3] Arnold Toynbee, "Unless We Learn to Love," *Guideposts* (March, 1966), p. 13.
[4] Pierre Teilhard deChardin, as quoted in John Powell's *Unconditional Love* (Niles, Ill.: Argus Communications, 1977), p. 97.

Chapter 13

[1] Lewis B. Smedes, "God's Noble Lady," *The Reformed Journal*, vol. 23, no. 1, p. 5.
[2] Paul C. Vitz, *Psychology as Religion: the Cult of Self-Worship* (Grand Rapids: Wm. B. Eerdmans Publishing Co., 1977), p. 93.
[3] Daniel Yankelovich, *New Rules: Search for Self-fulfillment in a World Turned Upside Down* (New York: Random House, Inc., 1981), p. xviii.
[4] Abraham Lincoln, as quoted in John Bartlett, *Familiar Quotations*, 8th. ed. (Boston: Little, Brown, and Co., 1955), p. 539.